IMPACT

THE ARMY AIR FORCES' CONFIDENTIAL PICTURE HISTORY OF WORLD WAR II

*Declassified and now published
for the general public for the first time
with fourteen new retrospective essays
by World War II leaders and journalists*

WINNING THE PACIFIC SKIES

James Parton, Consulting Editor

Sponsored by
THE AIR FORCE HISTORICAL FOUNDATION

Published by
NATIONAL HISTORICAL SOCIETY, HARRISBURG, PA.

Cover: 5th Air Force B-25s drop parafrag bombs on Japanese air strip at Dagua, New Guinea (*Impact,* April 1944)

Published by the National Historical Society
2245 Kohn Rd.
Harrisburg, Pa. 17105

Library of Congress Catalog Card Number: 79-91997

IMPACT: The Army Air Forces' Confidential Picture History
of World War II.

First edition

Printed in the United States of America

Air War Planning

Essays by

Major General Haywood S. Hansell Jr., U.S.A.F. (Ret.)
and
Lieutenant General Minoru Genda, Japanese Air Self-Defense Force (Ret.)

★1★
USAAF PLANS AND STRATEGIC EFFECTS

by Major General Haywood S. Hansell, Jr., USAF (Ret.)

About the author: *Son of an Army colonel, General Hansell gravitated naturally into a military career, becoming a Second Lieutenant in the Air Corps in 1929. For the next critical decade before World War II, he alternated staff and operational assignments. The most colorful was as a pilot of the aviation acrobatic team, "Three Men on A Flying Trapeze," which performed at the National Air Races in Cleveland in 1934. (Their leader was Captain Claire Chennault, later to win controversial fame with the Flying Tigers in China.) But his most important pre-war assignment was transferral in 1939 to the Intelligence Division, Office, Chief of Air Corps, in Washington.*

As a youth Hansell was nicknamed "Possum" because of his scoop-shaped nose and strongly pointed chin. In Intelligence that nickname rapidly earned a second meaning, indicative of his intuitive gift for out-thinking the enemy. More than any other officer, he was responsible for the basic Plans for Europe (AWPD-1 and -4) with which the Air Force entered World War II and which it followed (with a few adjustments) throughout. This was Possum's greatest achievement, as he rose in 1940 to Chief of the Operations Planning Branch, then as a Special Observer of the blitz in England for two months in 1941 before another year of planning on the Joint Strategic Committee of the General Staff in Washington.

In 1942 he returned to England to command an Eighth Air Force Bomb Wing and led some of the early missions (mostly against the U-boat pens in Lorient and St. Nazaire—targets the Air Force and he deplored as a diversion from more important objectives). In July 1943 he was named deputy commander in chief of the Allied Expeditionary Force, then recalled to Washington for more planning, now against Japan, as Deputy Chief of Air Staff. In November 1944 he took charge of the XXI Bomber Command based at Saipan. In that role he is shown here

briefing the 73rd Wing on Saipan for the first B-29 mission against the Musashino Aircraft Factory on the outskirts of Tokyo.

Rotated to the U. S. for more command and staff duties in 1945, Major General Hansell retired in 1946, was recalled to active staff duty in 1951 for two years during the Korean fight, and has since written two widely acclaimed books on military subjects.

—J.P.

As Hitler's armies cut their paths of victory through Europe, a mounting wave of apprehension engulfed the administration in Washington. Programs for expansion of the armed forces were presented to a reluctant Congress. One such program called for expansion of the Army Air Corps to fifty-four groups. It was presented to General George C. Marshall, Chief of Staff, early in 1940. On conclusion of the presentation by Major Laurence S. Kuter, General Marshall asked a penetrating question: "Why is this a fifty-four group program? Why not fifty-six, or sixty-four?"

As usual, General Marshall had gone directly to the root of the problem. What purpose was to be sought? What was the objective? Did it require fifty-four groups to attain that objective? Why? What was the strategic plan?

When the next opportunity arose for presentation of a major program, General Marshall's lesson was remembered. The planners asked themselves, what was expected to be achieved with the force? What was the purpose?

The next major program was the result of a presidential inquiry almost a year later. On July 9, 1941, some two weeks after Hitler had launched his massive attack on Russia, President Roosevelt addressed a letter to the Secretaries of War and the Navy, asking them to prepare an "estimate of overall production requirements required to defeat our potential enemies." There was, as usual, a short deadline for a reply.

The Joint Board of the Army and Navy was unable to agree upon an operational strategy, so each Department proceeded to prepare its own requirements.

The burden of preparing the War Department's reply fell upon the War Plans Division of the War Department General Staff. The War Plans Division proposed to estimate air requirements which were coordinated with ground requirements, and to append the air details to its report as "Annex 2 - Air Requirements." Colonel Harold Lee George, who had just been appointed Chief of the Air War Plans Division of the Air Staff, authorized three weeks earlier, asked that the responsibility for preparation of the Air Annex be placed upon his Division. General Henry H. Arnold made the necessary arrangements.

The War Plans Group of the infant Air War Plans Division consisted of two people: Lieutenant Colonel Kenneth N. Walker as Chief of the Group, and myself, Chief of the European Branch. Two chiefs and no Indians at all. Harold George devoted his full time to the project, and that made three. He succeeded in having Larry Kuter, on duty with G-3 of the General Staff, temporarily assigned to his Division. The four of us were faced with the task of preparing a strategic air plan for the conduct of war on a world-wide scale, and determining the forces that were needed to carry out such a plan. We would be constrained only by the physical capability of the United States to produce the recommended forces. In this latter regard we had the benefit of advice and counsel from the Air Material Command, with Major Max Schneider serving as a priceless liaison. By the time we got authority to proceed there were only seven days left for submission of the plan and report. We had one valuable asset going for us: we had spent years together as instructors in Bombardment and Air Force at the Air Corps Tactical School. We embraced a common concept of air warfare and we spoke a common language. I had spent the past year as head of the Strategic Air Intelligence Section of the Office, Chief of Air Corps, amassing and analyzing economic and industrial intelligence on the Axis Powers. That intelligence now proved a priceless asset.

Harking back to General Marshall's comments as well as our own teachings, we realized that the first requirement for our plan was a statement of purpose—a strategic objective. What should the air force try to achieve? What was the overall purpose? That was the fundamental keystone to plans, requirements and operations. But that purpose was not only missing from our instructions; it was also exceedingly hard to define.

The President's letter had called for defeat of our potential enemies. This was important guidance. Although he did not specify who our potential enemies were, there could be little doubt that they were the Axis Powers. His call for defeat cleared the air of any compromise objective. And we had two other guidelines which were significant. In passing the air requirement responsibility to the Air Staff, General Leonard T. Gerow of the War Plans Division had stipulated that the provisions of ABC-1 and Rainbow 5 should be followed. ABC-1 (American-British Conference No. 1) had taken place the previous February and its conclusions were incorporated in Rainbow 5 war plan in May of 1941. ABC-1 called for strategic offensive operations against the European Axis Powers as a maximum effort and strategic defensive operations in the Far East, with minimum diversion of forces from the main effort. And ABC-1 specifically stated: "Offensive measures in the European area will include a sustained air offensive against German military power, supplemented by air offensives against other regions under enemy control which contribute to that power."

But what should be the relationship of air power to the achievement of the national purpose and to the other forces? Air forces are flexible, but special types of aircraft are best suited to specific roles, and the selection and provision of aircraft would depend upon the major role to be assumed by air power. Even in regard to the defeat of the European Axis Powers there was a wide range of strategic air purposes to be considered:

1. Should the "sustained air offensive against German military power" seek to crush the war-making capability of the Third Reich by air warfare alone? If so, it would be necessary to destroy not only the industrial structure which supported the German armed forces, but also the industrial and economic structure which sustained the state itself. Or

2. Should the "sustained air offensive" seek to pave the way for invasion of the continent, with subsequent strategic air operations to continue to weaken the German ability to fight, in a continuing strategic air effort which was co-ordinated with the land campaign? Or

3. Should the sustained air offensive seek only to guarantee the success of the invasion, and devote its entire strength to the support and success of the land operations, which would become the sole reliance for final victory? And

4. What were the requirements for home defense?

The targets, the type and number of aircraft, and the organization of the air forces would vary with each of these options. Selection of a basic overall strategy was the *sine qua non* of air planning. And the problem was further compounded by the knowledge that the plan would have to take up the gauntlet of the War Department General Staff, culminating in a presentation to General Marshall. If General Marshall did not approve, the whole scheme simply would be discarded.

General Marshall was himself a far-sighted, broad-minded leader who had shown strong support for air power. But many Army officers still adhered to the official statement of Army doctrine which held that the sole mission of the Army Air Forces was the furtherance of the mission of the mobile army.

We knew that a strategy oriented solely to invasion and air support of ground warfare involved troublesome prospects, including long and perhaps disastrous delays. We knew that the War Plans Division had concluded that it would take two years to build a merchant marine capable of transporting and supplying the necessary ground forces. And it would take another six months to prepare them for invasion. An air offensive could be launched in half the time. Furthermore the War Plans Division was frank in admitting that Hitler's seasoned war machine would have to be seriously weakened before we could hope to defeat the Wehrmacht on the ground. In any event the German air forces would have to be defeated before an invasion could be undertaken. There was general agreement that a successful air offensive which would include defeat of the Luftwaffe must precede invasion. There was less unanimity as to what other purposes that air offensive should seek to accomplish.

We wrestled, as a group, with this basic and fundamental problem. The final solution was a statement of objective and a plan which leaned heavily toward victory through air power but which provided for air support of an invasion and subsequent combined operations on the continent *if the air offensive should not prove conclusive*. If the air offensive succeeded in destroying the German ability to support the war in bringing about capitulation, so much the better. The closer the air offensive came to finality, the greater the ease and the less the cost of invasion.

In the Air Plan we described the overall objective—the Air Mission—in these terms:

"A.   To wage a sustained air offensive against German military power, supplemented by air offensives against other regions under enemy control which contribute toward that power.

B.   To support a final offensive, if it becomes necessary to invade the continent.

C.   In addition to conduct effective air operations in connection with Hemisphere Defense and a strategic defensive in the Far East.

... there is a very high drain on the social and economic structure of the (German) state. Destruction of that structure will virtually break down the capacity of the German nation to wage war. The basic conception on which this plan is based lies in the application of air power for the break down of the industrial and economic structure of Germany. This conception involves the selection of a system of objectives vital to continued German war effort and to the means of livelihood of the German people, and tenaciously *concentrating all bombing* toward the destruction of those objectives.

. . . it is improbable that a land invasion can be carried out against Germany proper within the next three years. If the air offensive is successful, a land offensive may not be necessary."

The plan acknowledged that the German air force, especially the German fighter force, would have to be defeated before an invasion could be contemplated, and that such a defeat might also be necessary to the prosecution of the air offensive itself. Hence defeat of the German Air Force was accorded first priority among air objectives—an "intermediate objective of overriding importance," to take precedence over the Primary Air Objectives themselves.

As for Primary Objectives, the plan called for destruction and disruption of:

"A.   *Electric power:* disruption of a major portion of the German electric power system.
"Literally all the wheels of industry—civil as well as military—turn by electric power. The German electric power system, the second largest in the world, is known to be strained by the war effort. It is operating at 50% greater rate than that of Great Britain. All the armaments industries, including aircraft and engine plants, are directly dependent upon electric power." The electric power system might be likened to the neuro-muscular system of the human body. Disruption would vitiate controlled action. It was estimated that destruction of fifty targets would bring about collapse.

"B.   *Transportation*
"72% of German transportation is carried out by the railroads, 25% by canals and waterways, 3% by long-haul truckage."

The transportation system bore the same relationship to the German corporate body as the blood stream to the human body. Without a free flow of transportation, raw materials could not reach processing plants, manufactured parts and supplies could not reach factories and assembly plants, and finished products could not reach consumers, whether they be armed forces or civilian institutions. Forty-one targets, consisting of marshaling yards, bridges, canal locks and inland harbors were set up for the accomplishment of this objective.

"C.   *Petroleum and Synthetic Oil.*
"German motorized forces, the German Air Force, the German Navy, and a large block of German industry are dependent upon petroleum products. The blockade has cut off external sources other than Rumania, leaving the Reich heavily dependent upon a group of synthetic oil plants." Twenty-seven synthetic plants plus the refineries at Ploesti in Rumania were set up to accomplish this objective.

In summary, the plan called for destruction of the following target systems and targets:

German Air Force	18 airplane assembly plants
	6 aluminum plants
	6 magnesium plants
Electric Power	50 generating plants and switching stations
Transportation	47 marshalling yards, bridges and locks
Synthetic Petroleum	27 synthetic plants
TOTAL	154 targets

Bombing requirements for the destruction of each target, including repeat attacks to prevent restoration, were computed, using target dimensions and characteristics and tables of bombing probability.

Allowances were made for "aborts" and losses. The monthly rate of operations from British bases, based on weather records, was taken at five.

Finally, the total number of bomber sorties was computed, and the number of bombers needed to accomplish the entire task in six months at the rate of five missions per month was determined.

The key element in the entire plan was the proviso that the full bomber force should devote its entire strength to these targets for six months, after it had reached maturity. Invasion would follow if necessary. Requirements for hemisphere defense were also estimated.

The allowances for the defensive measures needed in the Far East were skimpy, to say the least. It was presumed that the U. S. Navy would be the primary agency for this requirement.

The air plan called for the offensive to be carried out primarily from bases in England, using B-17s and B-24s, and from bases in Northern Ireland and the vicinity of Cairo, Egypt, using B-29s. But the plan took cognizance of a contingency that bordered on disaster. Hitler's armies were slashing into Russia and soon would approach the gates of Moscow. If Russia should be defeated, Hitler could mass his forces for a final assault of Britain. And Britain might also succumb. In that case the British air bases would no longer be available. To meet that contingency the plan called for development and production of 44 groups of 4,000 mile bombers, B-36s, to continue the war from bases in the Western Hemisphere. But the strategic plan presumed that British bases would, in fact, continue to be available.

As a last resort, if these operations against industrial targets were not conclusive, the plan recommended direct attack on cities. But we never accepted attack on civilian populations as the primary method of air warfare.

We made provision for air support of an invasion of France if the air offensive should not be conclusive after six months of undiluted effort. The air plan provided additional air forces for air support of an invasion and for subsequent combined operations on the continent.

To carry out this strategy, the plan (referred to as Air War Plans Division I) called for some 63,000 operational aircraft, 180,000 officers and 1,940,000 enlisted personnel, a total of 2,120,000 men and women. Although strategic air operations could begin on a limited scale about a year after the outbreak of war, it was not expected that the air offensive force would be in place at full strength until about nine months later. Thus the full six months of strategic air warfare would end about two and a quarter years after the outbreak of war. The invasion force should be in place and ready to go by that time, if invasion should then be necessary. Even if effective German resistance was broken by the air offensive, an occupying force would be necessary in order to establish order, support an interim government, and insure adherence to peace terms. The opposition to such an occupying force might be considerable, but the enemy capacity for massive, organized resistance should be broken by that time.

The plan was completed, checked with General Arnold and Robert Lovett, and submitted to the War Department War Plans Division at literally the eleventh hour. It was not an impressive looking document. The pages were typed and mimeographed. Corrections were made in ink. The charts were black and white, hastily prepared and crudely pasted together. The entire War Plans document, including AWPD-1, was bundled off to the Government Printing Office.

Then followed a period of feverish preparation for presentation. We four were the presenters and Harold George drove us relentlessly in quest of perfection. We gave our presentations without notes, standing by charts and maps. A number of presentations were made to various staff organizations.

Finally, on August 30, we faced the crucial test. General Marshall, with Averell Harriman, the President's representative to Russia, General Arnold, General Muir S. Fairchild, several members of the General Staff and officials from war production listened to the presentation. There were questions, and some expressions of dissent, but General Marshall reserved his comment until all the others had been heard. Finally, he said, "I think the plan has merit. I should like the Secretary and the Assistant Secretaries to hear it."

That statement by General Marshall to General Arnold was a crucial turning point in the evolution of American air power.

Henry Stimson, the Secretary of War, was briefed on September 1 with General Marshall present. He showed a gratifying appreciation of the strategic concept. General Marshall offered encouraging comments. At last Mr. Stimson turned to Colonel George and said, "General Marshall and I like the plan. I want you gentlemen to be prepared to present it to the President."

A tentative date for the meeting with the President was set and intensive preparations for the presentation were under way when Pearl Harbor threw all arrangements into disarray. Loss of the opportunity to present to the President the detailed plans for strategic air warfare was a cruel disappointment. It is quite likely that the President's quick intelligence would have prompted him to make detailed inquiries, perhaps to have embraced the scheme with the same comprehension that characterized the reactions of General Marshall and Mr. Stimson. Lacking that presentation, Mr. Roosevelt never fully grasped the war-winning potential of air power.

Nonetheless, AWPD-1 became the basic blueprint for the creation of the Army Air Forces and the conduct of the air war. With the attack at Pearl Harbor the Air War Plans Division hastened to amend AWPD-1. The principal changes included requirements for additional air forces for the Pacific, to help compensate for the loss of U.S. capital ships, and the addition of a large number of air transports, since it was apparent that a heavy burden of overseas communications would have to be met by air. The new estimate was called AWPD-4.

Pearl Harbor brought two attendant consequences of immense importance. The Army-Navy war plans, which relied heavily upon the U. S. Fleet, had to be scrapped, leaving only the Air Plan, which was adopted almost by default. And Prime Minister Winston Churchill immediately cabled President Roosevelt and proposed a conference on Allied strategy. He proposed to bring with him the three British Chiefs of Staff and their key supporting staff members.

The President initially considered having the Joint Army-Navy Board meet with the British Chiefs of Staff Committee. But the Joint Board had no supporting Joint Staff, and there were only two primary members: the Chief of Staff of the Army and the Chief of Naval Operations. There were three members for Britain: the Chief of the Imperial General Staff, the First Sea Lord, and the Chief of Staff of the Royal Air Force. Air Chief Marshal Sir Charles Portal needed an "opposite number" on the American side. General Marshall proposed that the Commanding General, Army Air Forces, General H. H. Arnold, be appointed the American Air Chief as a full partner in the American Joint Chiefs of Staff. Arrangements were also made for a sup-

porting Joint Staff with four principal staff divisions: Joint Plans, Joint Intelligence, a Joint Strategic Committee and a Joint Logistics Committee. Later General Marshall recommended that Admiral William D. Leahy, a past Chief of Naval Operations, be appointed Chairman of the Joint Chiefs of Staff. The inclusion of Leahy completed a superb organization with which the President could work in his two war-time roles: as Commander in Chief he could work intimately and directly on the military conduct of the war; and as architect of national policy he could seek military advice and consultation on matters of international political scope. In the latter function the President did not bypass his principal civilian secretaries, the Secretaries of War, Navy and State. But he customarily included the Joint Chiefs in all meetings in which a military aspect, or the influence of military capability, might be considered. With the country at war this meant virtually every important meeting both at home and abroad.

When the British arrived in Washington, the "Arcadia" conference was carried out between December 22 and the end of the year. The grand strategy finally recommended by the Combined Chiefs of Staff, including provision for a combined British-American air offensive, was substantially that proposed by the Joint Chiefs, and the Combined Staff recommendations were adopted by the President and Mr. Churchill. The Arcadia Conference established the pattern for all the succeeding allied conferences: military proposals were worked up by the Joint Chiefs, generally after discussions with the President; broad and rather loose approval was obtained; final agreements were reached with the British Chiefs; and final approval was given by the President and the Prime Minister. The Chiefs of Staff carried out the approved directives.

The first threat to the air offensive against Germany came distressingly soon. The Prime Minister vigorously advocated an invasion of North Africa. This invasion would have to be supported with heavy bombers at the expense of the air offensive against Germany.

The Joint Chiefs took the position that an invasion of North Africa was militarily unwise. As General Marshall pointed out, it was a tangential thrust, at right angles to the proper axis of attack: the assault of Germany itself. The North African venture would swallow up vast military resources at the expense of the main effort, while accomplishing very little toward defeating the Reich in Europe.

General Arnold vigorously supported this position with special emphasis on the strategic air offensive against interior Germany. Admiral Ernest J. King, Chief of Naval Operations, believed that the margin of priority of Germany over Japan was very small and that any diversion of resources away from Germany should go to the Pacific, not to the Mediterranean.

The President weighed both the military arguments against diversion to North Africa and the political arguments for some visible evidence of military success. The air offensive against Germany was not well enough understood to meet political demand, nor were its true dimensions really understood by the President. The invasion of France was out of the question in 1942 and probably 1943. The President decided for the North Africa venture.

The Joint Chiefs protested vigorously but, having assured themselves that the President fully understood their military counsel and advice, they accepted the final decision and put their full energies behind the conduct of the military campaign. The whole episode was in the best tradition of American civilian/military relationship.

In August of 1942 the President asked for "an estimate of requirements to obtain air ascendency over our enemies." The answer was prepared in the Air Staff and became known as AWPD-42. The strategy remained the same as that of AWPD-1 but there was a minor change in targets. Submarine pens and bases were listed and given a high priority. This was eloquent testimony to the deadly threat of the German submarine campaign. In addition there was a dramatic shift in the requirements for Hemisphere defense. The threat to the Western Hemisphere had subsided somewhat and the large bomber and fighter forces which were to go into hemisphere defense were largely reassigned to the strategic air forces and the tactical air forces. The P-47, with its 2,000 horsepower engine, was found to have superb capabilities as a fighter-bomber. It became the mainstay of the Tactical Air Forces and Tactical Air Commands in Europe and the Mediterranean. The requirement for the B-36s was de-emphasized, reflecting the growing confidence in the security of the British Isles; and the B-29s were consigned to the Pacific, where their range would be needed in the air offensive against Japan.

Secretary Stimson, Assistant Secretary Lovett and Presidential advisor Harry Hopkins played important roles in the projection of air power as a war-winning strategy, and supported General Ar-

nold in respect to AWPD-1 and AWPD-42. The culmination of high-level policy in air warfare came with the policy statement known as the "Casablanca Directive."

The primary concern of the Casablanca Conference in January of 1943 initially pertained to surface operations, and the strategic air offensive was nearly submerged in the arguments concerning a cross-Channel invasion, recapture of Burma, and Pacific strategy.

General Arnold learned that the Prime Minister proposed to recommend to the President that the Eighth Air Force be directed to abandon daylight operations as too costly and to join RAF Bomber Command in night attacks of industrial areas of Germany. General Arnold sent for General Ira C. Eaker, Commanding General of the Eighth Air Force in England. General Eaker vigorously protested the abandonment of daylight bombing of selected targets. General Arnold arranged for General Eaker to meet with the Prime Minister.

In a singular and vital exposition, General Eaker persuaded Mr. Churchill to withdraw his opposition to daylight selective bombing by the Eighth Air Force, thus retaining the American concept of decisive strategic air warfare through destruction of selected vital targets. Although the daylight attack of selected targets was provoking bitter air fighting and producing heavy losses, General Eaker never wavered in his courageous support of the American strategy. He was a tower of strength in a sea of doubts.

The Casablanca Conference adopted a directive describing the objectives and strategy of both the RAF Bomber Command and the Eighth Air Force in a combined effort. The directive was prepared by one of the most gifted air strategists of the war, Air Vice Marshal Sir John Slessor, RAF.

The objective of the Combined Air Offensive was described in these terms: "To bring about the progressive destruction and dislocation of the German military, industrial and economic system and the undermining of the morale of the German people to a point where their capacity for armed resistance is fatally weakened."

This air strategy was a joint product of British and American airmen and it was approved by the Combined Chiefs and signed by both Mr. Churchill and Mr. Roosevelt at Casablanca on January 19, 1943. The Combined Chiefs of Staff finally agreed upon the Combined Bomber Offensive, the capture of Sicily and the postponement of further invasion until 1944. The President and the Prime Minister approved.

The Casablanca directive prompted preparation of an operational plan to carry it out. The operational plan for the Combined Bomber Offensive was prepared in General Eaker's headquarters. The target list was based upon target priorities prepared in Washington by the Committee of Operations Analysts and coordinated with the British Ministry of Economic Warfare. The new target list included all of the previous target systems except one, and added a vital new one: ball bearings. The one which was dropped was, unfortunately, electric power. The Committee of Operations Analysis had dropped electric power to priority thirteen, apparently on the grounds that it was beyond our capability to destroy and its effects would not be felt on the invasion beaches. Subsequent analysis shows that it probably would have been within our capability after the force reached maturity if strategic air power had not been unwisely diverted. Subsequent German testimony indicated that the operations initially planned against electric power would have produced catastrophic results.

The operational plans were sound enough, but the strategic air operations were constantly drained by the demands of Theater commanders for air support of ground-force campaigns. The resultant delay and diversion threw the strategic air war off schedule, with the result that only one of the strategic air objectives was attained before the invasion: defeat of the German air force. It was the *sine qua non* of all effective operations both land and air.

General Dwight D. Eisenhower demanded and received control of the U.S. Strategic Air Forces and RAF Bomber Command for support of the invasion. This was a reasonable requirement for a brief, critical period, while the invasion forces established themselves firmly in Normandy. But General Eisenhower retained control of those forces for six crucial months when they could have been most effective against systems in interior Germany. As a result of these delays and diversions, the massive air offensive against the selected primary targets did not really begin until September of 1944—ten months late and three months *after* the invasion.

This diversion of strategic air forces from their assigned mission was the more regrettable in light of the fact that General Eisenhower had ample tactical air forces for support of his land campaigns. The Ninth Air Force alone was larger than the entire Luftwaffe, which was fighting desperately on four fronts, and had already suffered a severe defeat.

The Ninth Air Force was superbly equipped, organized and led, and it did a magnificent job of providing air-ground support. The strategic air forces were equipped, trained and dedicated to an entirely different mode of air warfare and they made their greatest contribution in the field of their own peculiar capabilities. The strategic air forces were finally returned to their primary objectives in October. In the next four months the strategic air forces completed all the remaining strategic purposes originally proposed.

Effects of the strategic air war against Axis Europe

Following are brief digests of the effects of the air strategy including pertinent extracts from the Report of the U.S. Strategic Bombing Survey (USSBS), the civilian organization set up by General Arnold after the war to appraise the effect of the strategic air offensive.

1. *The German Air Force*

The long and bitter battle for control of the skies over Europe culminated in victory in the spring of 1944. There was no German air opposition to the landings in Normandy and the strategic air forces struck targets deep in Germany at will. The causes were destruction of plants, combat attrition, disruption of training and loss of aviation gasoline from attacks on the Rumanian oil fields and the synthetic plants in Germany. The intensity of the bitter fighting in the air is reflected in combat and operational losses. Excluding the Russian front, the Germans lost over 22,000 day fighters. The U.S. losses came to 12,000 bombers and a like number of fighters.

2. *Ball Bearings*

The target was right; the bombs were too small. There were two attacks in the fall of 1943. Factory buildings were demolished but heavy machinery survived. Albert Speer, the German Minister of Armaments Production, was asked after the war what would have happened if there had been concerted and continuous attacks on the ball-bearing industry. With heavier bombs, he replied: "Armaments production would have been crucially weakened after two months and after four months would have been brought completely to a standstill. In those days, we anxiously asked ourselves how soon the enemy would realize that he could paralyze the production of thousands of armaments plants merely by destroying five or six relatively small targets."

3. Synthetic Petroleum

This target system received thirteen per cent of total bombs dropped, almost all of it in late 1944 and early 1945. However, the system was extremely sensitive. An attack on May 12, 1944, sent production plummeting (see chart).

The oil campaign affected both the German Air Forces and Ground Forces. General Omar Bradley comments:

"With the debut of the German gamble in the Ardennes—lack of oil, which the strategic bombing campaign had enforced upon the enemy, told handsomely. The withdrawal of Sixth SS Panzer Army, begun in daylight on January 22, 1945, was marked mainly by successes of U. S. fighter bombers against its tanks and trucks. These successes, however, took place against a background of painfully exiguous oil reserve—with supply trucks being drained to fill the tanks of fighting vehicles—and a long pull to the distant loading stations.

"When the Allied breakthrough followed west of the Rhine in February, across the Rhine in March and throughout Germany in April, lack of gasoline in countless local situations was the direct factor behind the destruction or surrender of vast quantities of tanks and trucks and of thousands upon thousands of enemy troops.

"The effect spread to the Eastern Front as well; German forces restricted by lack of gasoline were unable to cope with the Russian onslaught. At the Baranov bridgehead, 1,200 German tanks, which had been massed to hold the position, were immobilized because they had no gasoline and were overrun by the Russians. Even Marshal Stalin agreed that the strategic air offensive against the oil resources played a vital part in making possible Russian victories in the East."

4. Transportation

This system received twenty-seven per cent of total bombs dropped. Although the attacks came late in the war, they were decisive.

The USSBS describes the situations as follows: "After the September and October attacks, it became entirely impossible for the railroad system to meet . . . transportation requirements. The evi-

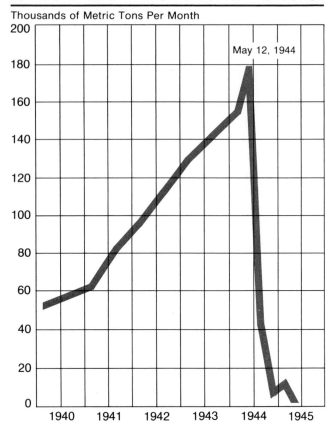

TOTAL SYNTHETIC AVIATION GASOLINE PRODUCTION

Thousands of Metric Tons Per Month

May 12, 1944

Effect of Strategic Bombing of German Synthetic Production of Aviation Gasoline.

dence indicates that the supply of critical components in the hands of manufacturers was quickly exhausted with a resulting severe impact on virtually all munitions and other finished products in late November and early December.

"The loss of transportation facilities completely disorganized the flow of basic raw materials, components and semi-finished materials, and even production was no longer possible."

The effects of the strategic air attacks upon rail and water transportation were almost exactly as envisioned in AWPD-1 and AWPD-42. Coal could not be moved to the steel plants and power stations, and the coal shortage interfered with rail movement. Component parts could not be moved to the assembly plants, and the assembly plants themselves could not operate.

The level of coal stocks for the railroads dropped to eighteen days in October 1944, to four and a half days in February 1945, and to less than one day in March. Under these conditions, orderly production was no longer possible. Steel production, for example dropped from more than nine million tons in the first quarter of 1944 to just over one million tons in the first quarter of 1945. The available capacity for economic traffic in Germany could no longer even hope to sustain war production, or to meet the needs of civil operations.

The Strategic Bombing Survey gave as one of its major conclusions: "Even if the final military victories that carried the Allied armies across the Rhine and the Oder had not taken place, armament production would have come to a virtual stand-still by May. The indications were convincing that the German armies, completely bereft of ammunition and motive power, would have had to cease fighting—*any effective fighting—within a few months.*" This was the intent of the strategic air plans. It should have been produced before the invasion. The diversion of the strategic air effort and the subsequent delay in effect, was a tragic mistake.

In his report to Hitler on March 15, 1945, Albert Speer stated flatly: "The German economy is heading for an inevitable collapse within four to eight weeks." Some time later, looking back at the strategic air assault, the U.S. Strategic Bombing Survey also included: "Allied air power was decisive in the war in western Europe". Noting that air power might have been employed more effectively at various times and places, the Survey's final report still emphasized: "Its power and superiority made possible the success of the (Normandy) invasion. It brought the economy which sustained the enemy's armed forces to virtual collapse, although the full effects of this collapse had not reached the enemy's front lines when they were overrun by Allied forces."

As for electric power, the target system that was dropped, there is no doubt of its importance, which was confirmed by the USSBS. From that point of view it should be noted for the future. But the feasibility of disrupting the system cannot be confirmed, since it was not attacked directly, and conclusions are necessarily speculative. Certainly it could not have been disrupted until the strategic air forces had finally reached their planned size, the German fighters had been defeated, and the available air power was literally overwhelming.

Speer has this to say on the subject: ". . . according to the estimates of the Reich, a loss of sixty per cent of the total power production would have sufficed to lead to collapse of the entire network. The destruction of the power plants would be the most radical measure as it would at once lead to a breakdown of all industry and public life. Destruction of fifty-six targets would produce this effect."

The chief electrical engineer in charge of design of the system volunteered this information: "The war would have been finished two years sooner if you concentrated in the bombing of our power plants . . ."

Strategic air war in the Pacific

AWPD-1 and AWPD-42 both contemplated a decisive strategic air offensive against Japan after the defeat of Hitler had been assured. Target systems were suggested. But there was a dearth of sound strategic intelligence about Japan's internal structure. Japanese security had been very tight. There was no detailed strategic air plan for Japan comparable to the strategic air plans against Germany.

The Theater air forces in the Pacific and Far East were literally starved initially because of the need to build up air forces for operations in the area of top priority—Axis Europe. Naval air forces fared much better. In spite of the European priority the Navy was able to build a very large carrier-based air force for operations in the Pacific, including over a hundred carriers of various sizes.

The Pacific area witnessed one surprising innovation of great importance: surface forces conducting a major campaign in support of air power. The Marianas Islands and Iwo Jima were captured as bases for the strategic air offensive of the B-29s. It was a new experience in military strategy and it bore the fruits of victory—a victory that came without the need of invasion.

Actually Japan had been beaten into a hollow facade by the Twentieth Air Force before the dropping of the atomic bombs.

The U. S. Strategic Bombing Survey has this to say on the subject of the defeat of Japan: "The bombing offensive was the major factor which secured agreement to unconditional surrender without an invasion of the Home Islands, an invasion that would have cost hundreds of thousands of American lives . . . Even without the atomic bombing attack, air supremacy over Japan could have exerted sufficient pressure to bring about unconditional surrender and obviate the need for invasion."

★2★
THE BENEFITS AND CONDITIONS OF SURPRISE ATTACK

by Lieutenant General Minoru Genda, Japanese Air Self-Defense Force (Ret.)

About the author: *Born in Hiroshima in 1905, Minoru Genda will be remembered by history as a key planner for the attack on Pearl Harbor and for subsequently rising to the highest post in the Japanese Air Service—Lieutenant General and Chief of Air Staff, Self Defense Forces (as the Japanese military structure was named after the war).*

Along the way, Genda graduated from the Naval Academy in 1924 and the Naval Staff College in 1937. That year he became Air Operations Officer in the Shanghai area and introduced new methods of mass, long-range operations by fighters. Skill and daring won his unit the nickname "The Genda Circus."

In 1938-1940 he was Assistant Air Attache in London, returning to staff and planning assignments in Japan. Genda shared Admiral Yamamoto's belief in the supremacy of naval air power and the importance of taking the offensive. After approval of the Pearl Harbor plan, Genda was appointed Air Operations Officer for the attack, supervised the flight training and participated in the highly successful onslaught. Six months later he also fought in the Battle of Midway, a Japanese disaster which marked the turning point of the war in the Pacific.

As Japan made its extraordinary post-war recovery, Minoru Genda was appointed Lieutenant General in 1956 and Chief of Air Staff in 1959. Retiring from the armed services, he was elected to the Upper House of the Diet in 1962 and re-elected in 1968 and 1974. The two pictures show him as a pilot in the Japanese air force and as a Member of the House of Councillors in 1978.

—J.P.

It was in 1921 that I entered the Japanese Naval Academy. That same year, the Naval Limitations Conference was held in Washington, and Japan was restricted to a force of capital ships and aircraft carriers no greater than sixty per cent of those of the United Kingdom and the United States respectively.

The history of combat teaches us that there are instances in which victory has been won at a ratio of seventy per cent but none at the handicap of sixty per cent. This was the reason the Japanese Navy abandoned its tradition of attack on sight, handed down from the time of Admiral Heihachiro Togo—who surprised the Russians at Port Arthur in 1904 and annihilated them in the Tsushima Strait in 1905. Instead, we adopted the strategic concept, which requires great skill, of the so-called "tactic of gradual decrease."

The essence of the tactic of gradual decrease can be described as follows: An American fleet making an advance into the western Pacific Ocean would first be intercepted, observed and followed by a submarine group and would be subjected to surprise attack when a favorable opportunity presented itself. If the fleet drew closer, it would be further subjected to a night-time torpedo attack by an advance force composed of a destroyer and cruiser group. Once the strength of the American force had been worn down until it was almost equal to that of our force, decisive action would be taken in order to annihilate the remaining American force at a single stroke.

The swift growth of air power after 1921 added a new dimension and greater validity to this planning concept.

In the twenty-year period from the time I entered the Navy until 1941, the Japanese Navy was outfitted and trained entirely on the basis of this concept. In 1936, the doctrine of air supremacy was proposed by myself and Vice Admiral (then Captain) Takijiro Ohnishi, later to be the creator of the Kamikaze Special Attack Force. However, this amplification of the tactic of gradual decrease was not accepted by the Navy authorities.

Despite all our efforts to breathe life into the Japanese Navy, the results of all of the training that we had conducted were not in the least satisfactory. This was to be expected in the light of historical precedent. The American and Japanese navies were established on the basis of similar strategic concepts, and although they differed in numerical strength by the factor of six to ten they were of the same character. If Japan did not adopt the doctrine of air supremacy, then they would come to differ in terms of the basic concept of maritime strategy. When we conducted "war games," or exercises, assuming that one side was the Japanese Navy and the other the American Navy, both following similar strategic concepts and structures of forces and with the tacticians of both having received similar educations, the side with the greater numbers always won.

To escape this predicament, Admiral Isoroku Yamamoto, Minister of the Navy from 1938, devised the Pearl Harbor attack. By means of surprise attack at the outset of hostilities, the ratio of Japanese and American capital ships could be equalized at a single stroke. However, such a strategy had never before been conceived of in the Japanese Navy, nor had studies and exercises concerning it been conducted. Furthermore, it would be extremely dangerous. If it failed, both the leaders and their men would be lost, as well as large forces of ships and planes.

What Admiral Yamamoto had planned was to strike a blow sufficient to render it impossible for American capital ships to advance in the western Pacific within a minimum period of five months—that is, the period up to the completion of our occupation operations in what we called "the South Seas resources zone." This was the vast area to the south of Japan then known as the Dutch East Indies, Indochina, Malaysia and Australia—a region with oil, rubber and other war resources Japan needed. We also needed to capture control of the thousands of islands and miles of jungle to extend the defense perimeter of Japan itself.

I was ordered to study this strategy and the Pearl Harbor plan in the utmost secrecy. I concluded that the following three factors were basic conditions:

1. The attack must be administered by a decisive

blow in which Japanese victory would be determined at a single stroke.

2. Absolute secrecy must be maintained.

3. The morale and training of those taking part, and the aircraft crewmen in particular, must be maintained at the highest level.

At that time, the main force of the American Pacific fleet made frequent use of Pearl Harbor. From a strategic standpoint, this would be the starting position of the American fleet in the event that hostilities broke out between Japan and the United States: before a tiger attacks its prey, it contracts its body in preparation for its leap.

Now, Pearl Harbor is located far to the east of the middle of the Pacific Ocean, being 3,400 nautical miles from Tokyo Bay and 2,100 nautical miles from San Francisco. In addition, the Hawaiian Islands had been strengthened and fortified as bases of the U. S. armed forces. We could not sensibly plan an invasion or the capture of such a distant, strongly defended fortress.

At any cost, a decisive lightning attack determining victory at a single stroke would have to be made. A major element in such a victory would be a daytime attack. In the case of Pearl Harbor, the geographical features of which were only partially familiar to us, a lightning night-time attack could not be made. There was too high a probability that the bombing and torpedoing would not be accurate. Consequently, we would have to take advantage of the darkness of night to approach the enemy, take off from the carriers at dawn and attack during the daytime.

According to our data, the water depth of Pearl Harbor was twelve meters, and for that reason the depth of the guided torpedos would have to be controlled to within twelve meters. (The launching height commonly used at that time by our navy was one hundred meters, and depth was sixty meters.) Study and exercises were carried out over a ten-month period in order to minimize such difficulties. The problem was solved on October 10, 1941, one week before the task force departed from the Japanese mainland.

Under ordinary conditions it is easy to maintain the morale of crewmen. However, since secrecy made it impossible to inform them of the actual tactical objectives, extraordinary efforts were necessary to keep their enthusiasm high during preliminary training in torpedo attacks on anchored ships. For this purpose, we selected particularly distinguished commanders, unmatched in the Japanese Navy, as our task force leaders, capable men whom everyone would follow unconditionally. They were informed of the task force plan on October 1, 1941.

We devoted our greatest efforts to maintaining secrecy. An operation like the Pearl Harbor attack could not be brought off unless it was a surprise attack, and the precondition for surprise attack is the maintenance of secrecy.

Of the cases of battles in which success had been achieved in taking the enemy by surprise, I chose three models. The first was the storming of the Taira armed forces from the rear by Minamato Yoshitsune in the battle of Ichi-no-tani in 1184; the second was the attack on Okehazama by Oda Nobunaga in 1560; and the third was the crossing of the Alps by Napoleon in the battle of Marengo in 1800. Specifically, all of them were strategies so filled with danger and so lacking in common sense that almost no one supported them in advance. The driving forces behind them were the judgments of the commanders that victory could be won and the incomparable will of these commanders.

The Pearl Harbor plan was, of course, not made known outside of the extremely limited group of those concerned with it. But almost everyone, from the operations section at General Headquarters to the headquarters of the first-line aircraft carrier fleets that would have to carry out the attack, was opposed to it. There was a conference in which it was stated that such an operation could not be carried out unless a majority expressed approval.

At the time of the final map exercises on board the flagship *Nagato* in October 1941, the atmosphere worsened. There were some who proposed that the Hawaiian Operation be abandoned entirely, and others who felt that the allotted troop strength should be reduced from six carriers to three, those with long cruising ranges.

In the midst of these conditions, Admiral Yamamoto issued his historic instructions to those involved in the Hawaiian Operation. He took the platform, seeming to fix his eyes angrily on each person present, and declared in a resolute tone, "There are various opinions concerning the Hawaiian Operation, but as long as I am Commander in Chief of the joint fleet this operation will proceed. I do not wish to hear any further discussion about this question in the future. As long as it is going to be done, I shall adopt the plan which satisfies the men taking part in it."

I had been accorded the honor of attending the meeting together with those who were taking part in the exercises, and when I heard his instructions I not only sensed the overpowering intensity of Admiral Yamamoto but also thought, "I have heard about the speech and conduct of many great commanders, and I suspect that they must have been just like him."

In these instructions—straightforward and expressive of will—by Admiral Yamamoto, there were two extremely important points in respect to him as a commander. First, he made the objectives of the operation extremely clear and expressed them with indomitable will. Second, although he did not permit any criticism of the objectives of the operation, he entrusted the details of its execution to the discretion of his subordinates.

Selection of the route of advance was one such important decision facing the task force headquarters in the course of drawing up plans for the operation. The task force was made up of a large force of over thirty vessels, including, in addition to the six mother aircraft carriers which were the main force, two battleships, other light warships and supply vessels. If the advance were discovered during its course, not only would the plan be frustrated but there would also be a great danger of being met by a devastating counterattack. It was absolutely necessary to carry out the advance over several thousand nautical miles without meeting either an American vessel or a merchant vessel of a neutral nation.

After due consideration, the course that I selected was one that passed to the south of the Aleutian Islands and then turned straight south from a point several hundred nautical miles directly north of the island of Oahu. There was a clear reason for this.

From a survey of past records over several decades, I found that because of the extremely rough seas in the northern Pacific Ocean during winter, most merchant vessels crossing the Pacific Ocean passed to the north of the Aleutian Islands, while the American fleet hardly ever carried out exercises on the seas north of Hawaii during winter. In addition, according to data we obtained from our intelligence division, patrols by American military aircraft were limited almost entirely to the sea south of Hawaii.

No one would approve adoption of the northern course. The commander the task force, Vice Admiral Chuichi Nagumo, was in the forefront of those opposing it. His reasons were that the rough seas would hamper navigation of the vessels, and moreover that they would make transfer of supplies absolutely impossible at sea.

Despite such strong opposition, I became more than ever confirmed in my view that we must take the northern course. The reason for this was simple: Since both the Japanese and the American naval officers had received similar educations, a course that was thought to be unsuitable by Japanese officers would also be thought to be unsuitable by American officers. My views eventually prevailed.

As everyone knows, the actual attack did achieve almost total surprise as well as almost total success. The only major failure was caused by the unforeseen coincidence that the U. S. aircraft carriers were not in port as we had expected. They were conducting routine maneuvers at sea and thus escaped the heavy damage or destruction we inflicted on the American battleships.

Hence, the U. S. carrier force remained intact and able to fight the critical battles of the Coral Sea and Midway. The latter may truly be said to have been the turning point of the war in the Pacific—a great U. S. victory made possible not only by the absence of the carriers from Pearl Harbor on December 7, 1941, but by American breaking of the Japanese code.

On balance, however, the Pearl Harbor attack achieved its primary strategic goal. Had it not been carried out, Japan might have had to abandon its invasion of the "South Seas Resources Zone" in mid-course.

To our children and grandchildren we should recall the dictum written in the fourth century B. C. by the great Chinese military tactician, Sun Tzu: "If you understand your opponent and also understand yourself, you need not fear a hundred battles; if you understand yourself but not your opponent, you will win and lose by turns; but if you understand neither your opponent nor yourself, the war will be lost."

The political leaders of Japan in 1941 misunderstood this principle. On the basis of the situation at that time, Japan should not have gone to war with the United States. Our leaders should have altered the course of Japan's policy toward mainland China. But whether we carried out the attack on Pearl Harbor or did not, it was our destiny to be defeated.

IMPACT

B-29 . . . See p. 22

DISTRIBUTION: SQUADRONS

OFFICE OF THE
ASSISTANT CHIEF OF AIR STAFF, INTELLIGENCE
WASHINGTON, D. C.

Vol. 2   No. 2
FEBRUARY, 1944

IMPACT is a medium for the dissemination, in graphic form, of air intelligence and correlated subjects. It presents information on the results of our operations against the enemy. So that Air Force units in one theater may be informed of how units in another meet specific problems, pertinent data on the operations themselves is also included.

The publication as a whole is classified CONFIDENTIAL so that a maximum of data can be included but it is intended that it be read by every member of our armed forces to whom it may be of value.

Material which members of the Army Air Forces in the field believe suitable for publication should be forwarded, with descriptive text and special annotations when necessary, through regular channels marked for the attention of IMPACT.

IMPACT

Contents—February, 1944

CLASSIFICATION: A combination of text and pictures or a revealing sequence of pictures is sometimes classified higher than are individual photos. For units which may use the pictures alone for instructional purposes, the following page by page list is published (unless otherwise noted, all text is CONFIDENTIAL):

COVER—CONFIDENTIAL

1, 2—CONFIDENTIAL

3—TOP, RESTRICTED; BELOW, UNCLASSIFIED

4—CONFIDENTIAL

5—TOP, UNCLASSIFIED; BELOW, CONFIDENTIAL

6, 7—ANNOTATED PICTURES, CONFIDENTIAL; OTHERS UN-CLASSIFIED

8, 9—CONFIDENTIAL

10—TOP, CONFIDENTIAL; BELOW, UNCLASSIFIED

11, 12, 13—CONFIDENTIAL

14, 15, 16—RESTRICTED

17, 18—CONFIDENTIAL

19, 20, 21—RESTRICTED

22, 23, 24, 25, 26, 27—CON-FIDENTIAL

28, 29—UNCLASSIFIED

30, 31—RESTRICTED

32, 33—UNCLASSIFIED

34, 35—CONFIDENTIAL

36, 37, 38, 39, 40, 41, 42—RESTRICTED

43—UNCLASSIFIED

44—BOMB PLOTS CONFIDENTIAL; OTHERS, UNCLASSIFIED

45, 46, 47, 48, INSIDE BACK COVER—CONFIDENTIAL

BACK COVER—UNCLASSIFIED

CONFIDENTIAL

AIR WAR CATCHES UP TO THE COMIC STRIPS

ROCKET BURSTS SURROUND B-17 OVER EMDEN; ME-210s ARE COMING IN AGAIN FOR CANNON-FIRING RUN

Skies over Europe Exhibit Some Weird and Bizarre Sights

"Ingenious but fantastic." "Overstimulating to the children." These and similar comments, accompanied by grave head-shakings, have greeted comic strip artists who, even recently, dreamed up scenes such as those on pages 1, 2 and 3.

Above is the first picture to reach the United States of rocket bursts—these projectiles, usually fired from twin-engined fighters, are more than twice as large as 88 mm anti-aircraft shells and have a lethal bursting radius of about 100 feet. They were described in IMPACT, Vol. I, No. 8. It would be comforting to report that rockets are merely the hare-brainchild of a crackpot inventor but they constitute an extremely practical and lethal weapon. Rocket-bearing planes knocked down many of the 60 bombers and five escorting fighters that were lost on the mission of 11 January. The Germans have an equally bizarre weapon in the radio-controlled glider bomb and no one knows what they will produce next.

On our own side, radar has produced many miracles including the technique of bombing through the overcast using sur-realistic looking smoke markers (see following pages and IMPACT, Vol. II, No. 1). We have announced that the British-invented jet-propelled fighter plane is in production here so perhaps Buck Rogers had better be brought back from the 25th century before his equipment becomes obsolete, even by 20th century standards.

PROBABLE ROCKET (indicated by arrow) speeds through air before explosion. Formation was over St. Dizier, France.

Continued on next page

SMOKE MARKER goes straight down from a preceding path-finder plane which has located the target by means of radar devices. This guides the incoming B-17s in releasing their bombs. Arrow indicates bursting point of smoke bomb.

WORTHY OF DANTE'S INFERNO—coils of smoke from parachute markers (1) zigzag to earth while other smoke markers (2) plunge down. They mix with the Bremen smoke screen of 20 December and bomb bursts (3).

SMOKE FROM FIRES SET BY PREVIOUS BOMBS, coming up through 10/10 clouds, is a startling but satisfying sight

to B-24 crews over Bremen. This was on 16 December, when 131 B-24s and 397 B-17s dropped 1,520 tons of bombs.

LIKE A BUNDLE OF MATCHES, as indeed they are, 500-pound clusters of incendiaries plunge through 10/10 clouds on

a big Kiel shipyard on 13 December. One of the containers is seen. For results of this and the Bremen missions, turn page.

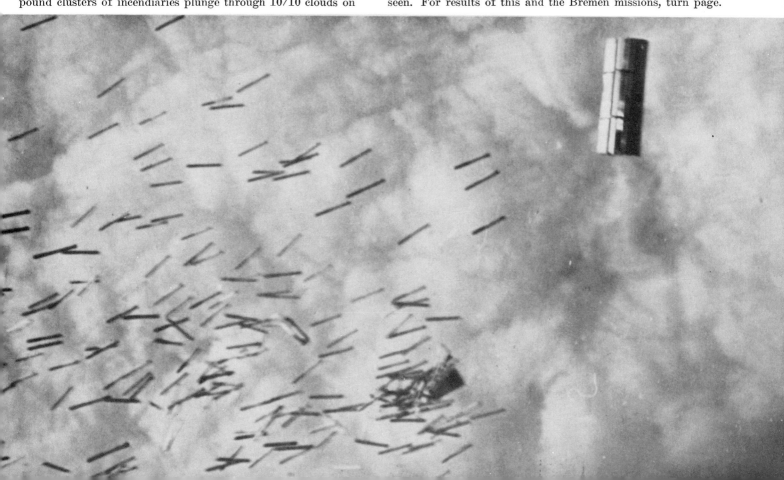

Results of Bombing Through Overcast

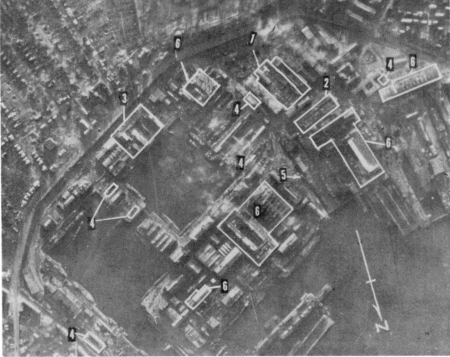

◄ BREMEN, After: Some of the damage caused by the 8th Bomber Command attacks, including those of 16 and 20 December in which almost 1,000 heavy bombers dropped 2,600 tons of bombs, is shown around Hafens 1 and 2 (left). In addition Swedish reports say that six ships were sunk as well as barges. Warehouses and dock facilities destroyed are circled. At right a petroleum refinery is still afire.

◄ KIEL, Before: A top priority target, the Deutsche Werke Kiel A. G., an important shipbuilding yard, is shown as it appeared on a clear day last summer. When the time for the mission of 13 December arrived, however, there was a 10/10 cloud cover, so the 256 B-17s and 99 B-24s which reached the target, using overcast technique, dropped the following: 1,620 GP bombs, 500 pounds each, fused at 1/10 second nose and 1/40 second tail; 4,670 hundred-pound incendiary and 973 incendiaries clusters, 500 pounds each, of which some are seen falling on the preceding page. Pathfinder planes marked target with gratifying results (below).

◄ KIEL, After: A reconnaissance photo shows damage as follows: (1) workshop and storage building 80% gutted; (2) carpenters' workshop gutted; (3) factory workshop and boat-building shop two-thirds gutted; (4) denotes a number of buildings, all almost completely destroyed; (5) hit on hull of submarine under construction; (6) other damage, including hits on the turbine engine and engineering workshops and plate sheds and in the vicinity of the central power station. Another concentration of damage, not shown, is in the business center of town and includes the town hall. Target escort was provided by a group of P-38s and withdrawal was covered by a group of P-51s. We lost only two B-17s and one B-24. Enemy opposition was weak but we shot down seven planes, probably accounted for three more and damaged 17. The submarine hit is one of the 500-ton type, which is the m in product now of these yards. They formerly turned out such warships as the Gneisenau, the Luetzow and the aircraft carrier, Graf Zeppelin.

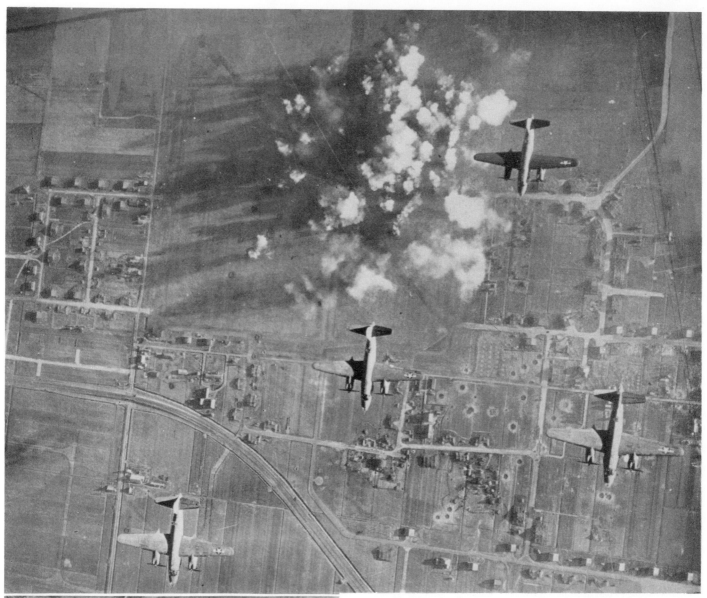

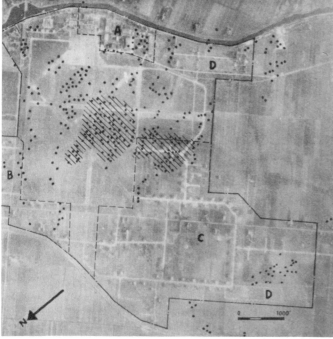

Old-Fashioned Visual Way Still Good; Here's Sample of Tactical Pasting by 9th AF

A systematic beating is being administered to the western coast of Europe by the U. S. 9th Air Force, now operating out of the United Kingdom as part of the Allied tactical set-up. Military installations, such as Schipol airport at Amsterdam (shown on this page), are the targets. These missions continue and expand the work of the 8th Air Support Command (IMPACT, Vol. I, No. 8), which was absorbed in the formation of the 9th. During the attack on 13 December 199 B-26s, some of which are pictured above, dropped 780 thousand-pound bombs. Altitudes varied from 15,900 to 23,000 feet. In the bomb plot at the left dots indicate well-defined bursts while diagonal lines show areas of heavy concentrations. Letters refer to (A) hangars and repair shops, (B, C) dispersal, (D) ammunition.

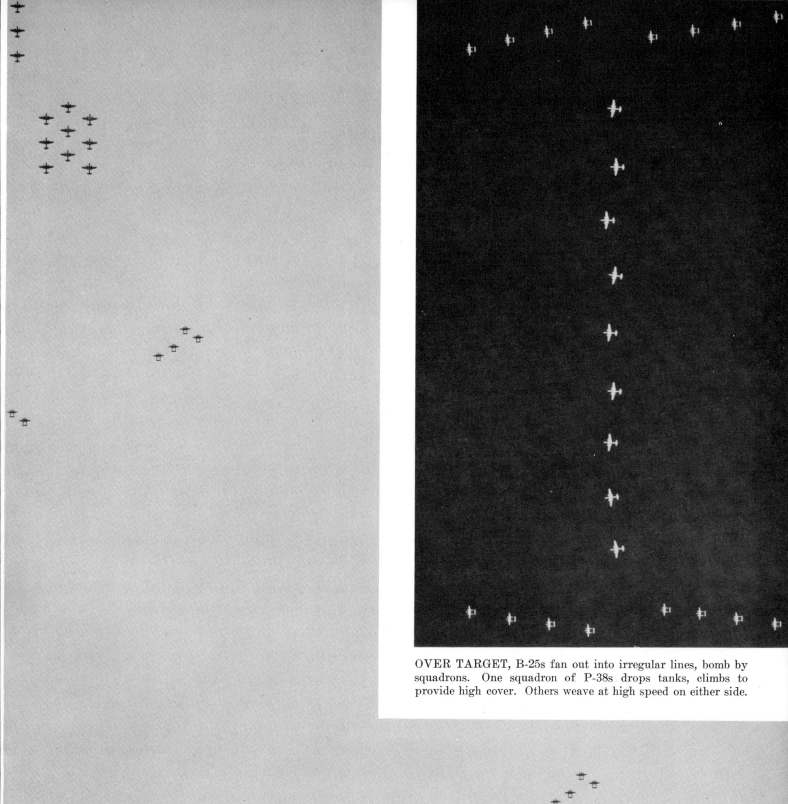

OVER TARGET, B-25s fan out into irregular lines, bomb by squadrons. One squadron of P-38s drops tanks, climbs to provide high cover. Others weave at high speed on either side.

Rabaul Harbor — Sample of Results from 5th AF Tactics

JAP SHIPS totaling 114,572 tons were either sunk or damage on mission of 2 November to Rabaul. How some of them were lost is shown in this series of photos. Above, a 1,000-lb. bomb sends stern of 4,217-ton Hokuyo Maru (1) skyward.

10,380-TON TRANSPORT, Hakusan Maru (5) burns fiercely from direct hit amidships. Tokyo Maru (4), 6,485 tons, was badly damaged; Gosei Maru (3), 1,950 tons, destroyed; Hayasaki (2), 1,500 tons damaged. Blast (1) develops.

NACHI CLASS CRUISER (8), 10,000 tons, desperately tries to get up speed, but was damaged later. Chogei, (9) 5,160-ton sub tender, was damaged, as were two 3,800-ton motor vessels, (6) and (7). No. 1, now settling, is total loss.

CRUISER HEADS into hail of bombs as 800-ton minecraft (10) scuttles out, only to be badly strafed later. Yamabiko (11), a 6,798-ton destroyer tender, was damaged from direct hit shown. Smoke around town is from phosphorus bombs.

HARUNA MARU (12), 1,550 tons, still afloat here, was destroyed and sunk by a later wave of B-25s. Lyons Maru (13), 7,000 tons, and Onoe Maru (14), 6,667 tons, were damaged. Of 40 ships in harbor, only 10 escaped injury.

For the PHOTO

Invasion Defenses

Slide your stereoscope from the coast at the top of the pair of pictures at the left down through the rest of this position. This is a sample of the way the Germans have the western coast of Europe organized against invasion. Photo Interpretation has already played an important part in revealing the enemy's defenses and will continue to play a big part as the situation develops. On these pages, in sketches and oblique and stereo photographs, are typical coastal installations. The defense ranges from simple trenches and barbed wire to elaborate structures of concrete and steel which house long range guns. Approaches to beaches contain minefields and underwater obstacles. The beaches themselves have anti-tank and anti-personnel mines. Wire entanglements are on beaches, in gulleys and on cliffs.

Gun emplacements and pillboxes of brick and concrete may be found on dikes, inside of sand dunes and among the cliffs. Concrete emplacements are located under the promenades along sea walls. Tank turrets on concrete are located on moles or the whole tank buried in the sand and used as a pillbox. Many private homes have become concrete and steel gun emplacements without altering the exterior appearance. In The Hague a mile of three-story houses were demolished for an anti-tank ditch.

Each position can contribute predetermined fire for the defense of its own ground and for covering the dead spaces of neighboring positions. The strong points, the Germans hope, form an irregular pattern of defense in depth, which commands all critical terrain.

COASTAL DEFENSE BATTERY near Cape Gris Nez, France, has massive concrete and steel construction. Small arms positions, wire and mine fields surround it.

ANTI-TANK walls shown in the vertical stereo pair above and the

INTERPRETER

WATER-FILLED, these anti-tank ditches are on the landward side of Ijmuiden, The Netherlands, to protect against attack from rear. Circles denote probable anti-tank guns.

HEAVY FOUR-GUN antiaircraft battery near Ostend—this is defended from local attack by barbed wire, trenches, machine gun emplacements and probable concrete pillboxes.

ANOTHER TYPE of defense position is this battery of four heavy and two light antiaircraft guns on concrete towers behind a dike at Emden, Germany. Towers appear 40-50 feet high.

oblique photograph at the right are constructed across the ends of streets next to beaches as a defense against landing parties. Those shown in the photos, near Dunkerque, are several feet thick. Some of these are 20 ft. high.

FLAK: DON'T LET IT GET YOU DOWN

SPLIT THREE WAYS by flak, this B-17 was lost over Bremen. Top left: tail assembly. Center right: starboard wing with two motors. Lower right fuselage upside down. Freak accidents like this are too rare to be much of a problem.

Two Schools of Thought Exist on Problem of Evading AA Fire

These pictures, here and on the next pages, show some extraordinary accidents when our bombers have been caught by enemy flak. They are not common occurrences, but they serve as a reminder that flak is not confetti and should be approached with proper caution. The standard methods of flak evasion were shown in IMPACT (Vol. I, No. 8). Another school of thought, while agreeing that evasive action is desirable in many cases, maintains that it should not be taken between the Initial Point and the Bomb Release Point on heavily defended targets. When flak is fired from 100 to 300 guns the pattern is so widespread, it is argued, that no formation using normal evasive action can dodge it. In other words, in this limited area you can't get away from flak anyway, so don't sacrifice time and accuracy by weaving around. In the 8th Bomber Command, groups which have used these new tactics have reported no appreciable increase in casualties, while they have definitely increased bombing accuracy on some targets. The three examples of flak casualties which follow occurred before the formations reached the Initial Point.

BURSTS ABOVE CLOUDS indicate that this is continuously pointed flak attacking B-24s on December mission to Cognac.

RIGHT WING MAN of higher element blows up. In this type of flak, altitude or course should change every 30 seconds.

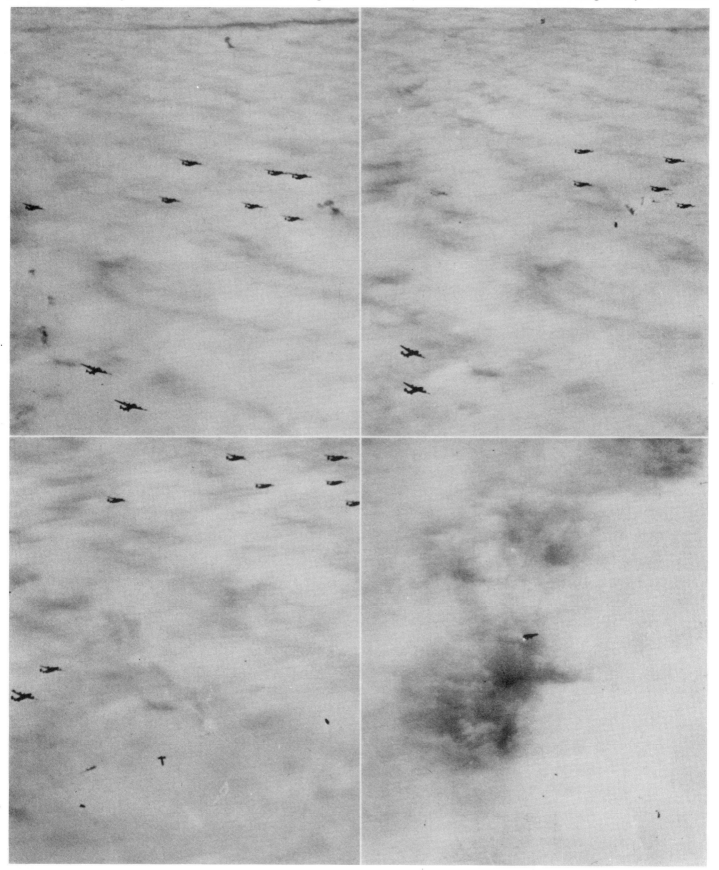

PLANE FALLS APART, with tail in lower foreground. Note that formation, except for two stragglers, continues.

FALLING WRECKAGE of plane drops into overcast. In heavy cloud cover continuously pointed flak is radar-controlled.

Continued on next page

Anzio

tuno

AIRFIELDS, RAIL LINES AT ROME OUT BY D-DAY

ROME, Guidonia Airfield: Another Rome airfield gets a pre-invasion trouncing. Many buildings, including four hangars, suffered direct hits. Explosions are shown among the hangars. Thirty-six B-17s from the 15th Air Force made the attack with 105 tons of 500-pound bombs from 19,700 to 23,000 feet on 13 January.

VELLETRI: Clouds of bomb smoke twist upward from this railroad junction just back of the Anzio beachhead. On D-day 48 B-25s and 34 B-26s dropped 144 tons of bombs on various junctions around Velletri—an enemy strong point.

Continued on next page

APPROXIMATE NORTH

0   1 MILE

BUT—WALLOP AT BARI SHOWS THAT GAF IS STILL POTENT

The Italian port of Bari, major Allied Adriatic docking point, was attacked on the evening of 2 Dec. by 30 German aircraft releasing mines and bombs. Seventeen cargo vessels were destroyed, 1,000 men killed, and two British warships damaged. Dropping of metallic strips of "window," which jammed ground radar, prevented effective air interception.

PAIR OF MERCHANT VESSELS burn fiercely the day after the bombing. Holocaust was started by direct hits on two ammunition carriers which exploded, spreading fires rapidly. Some ships still burned on 4 December.

BARI SKYLINE is illuminated by fires, searchlights, tracers and flares (irregular lines) dropped by a force of 30 Ju-88s. No enemy planes were downed by night fighters or antiaircraft.

SIXTEEN DAYS LATER Bari waterfront was still clogged with a mass of oil-soaked wreckage, testifying to costly losses of supplies. Note reflections in oil-covered water below.

lower turret guns on earlier models, and two in new tail turret. Speed and range has not been affected by new guns.

TWO .50 CALIBER TAIL GUNS and new turret in the B-25J represent latest modification. Gunner sits comfortably.

FLEXIBLE TAIL GUN and enlarged tail section were added to B-25D, shown in this interior view. Gunner lies on mattress.

WAIST GUN, first installed by cutting an opening in the side of a B-25D, gave wide angle of fire and afforded new protection from below. Improved waist guns are now on B-25J.

EVOLUTION OF A B-25

The evolution of a plane follows the law of nature. Hundreds of adaptations are tried out to meet new combat conditions. Only the fittest survive. Adapt or perish is the rule.

A case in point is the B-25J, the newest model of the B-25, which has evolved from the tips of many combat crewmen, Air Service engineers, and the manufacturer. It carries the heaviest armor of any medium bomber except for its stablemate, the B-25H which boasts of four guns and a cannon in its all-metal nose. The B-25J, with plexiglass nose for the bombardier, is slated for operation in the Asiatic theater.

Most of the B-25J's modifications evolved on earlier models. The double package guns, for example, were first tried out by P. I. "Pappy" Gunn in the early days of the New Guinea campaign when he simply wired .50 caliber machine guns to each side of the fuselage. Other innovations, such as the new waist guns and the enlarged tail section, were installed by the Air Service Command on the B-25D for use by the 321st Bomber Group in North Africa. The success of this group, which lost no planes to enemy aircraft in 25 missions, did more than anything to "sell" the new fixtures. In this article you see some of these historic modifications when they first appeared, later to become standard on the B-25J.

For The PHOTO-INTERPRETER

Facts on Formosa

Photo-interpreters are digging out the facts about Formosa, now that this important part of the Japanese empire is on the regular bomber and reconnaissance routes. Studies of its four chief airfields by a Photo Intelligence Detachment of the 14th Air Force indicate that without doubt Formosa is used as an aircraft and aircrew clearing area for the Southwest Pacific and Southeast Asia. On Heito field a maximum of 130 planes were visible on 10 January, 1944; at Okayama 113 on 12 January; the greatest number on Tainan was 66 on 17 November and at Shinchiku 88, mostly Nells, just before our Thanksgiving day bombing. In every photo cover the number of aircraft is in excess of local needs.

The sketches, prepared at 14th AF headquarters, are of typical and unusual installations. Common to all are the hangars and hangar-shops. The radio station in its general layout is the same at all the fields, the variance being in the design of the building and the placement of the towers.

The permanent status of these fields is shown by luxuries such as swimming pools and athletic fields.

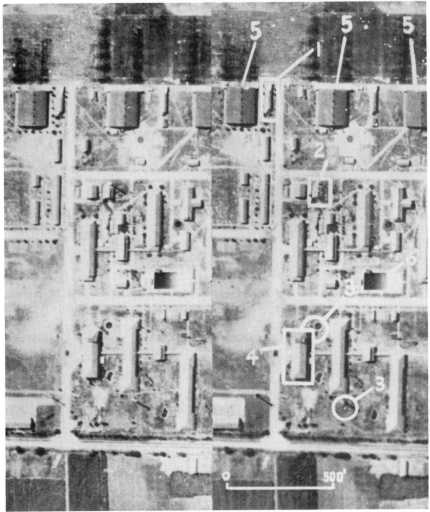

SECTION OF FIELD at Tainan shows (1) control tower, (2) power plant, (3) radio towers, (4) radio-administration building, (5) peaked roof hangars and (6) swimming pool. All except latter are shown in oblique sketches.

1. CONTROL TOWER

3. & 4. TOWERS, RADIO-ADMINISTRATION CENTER

2. POWER PLANT

5. PEAKED ROOF HANGAR

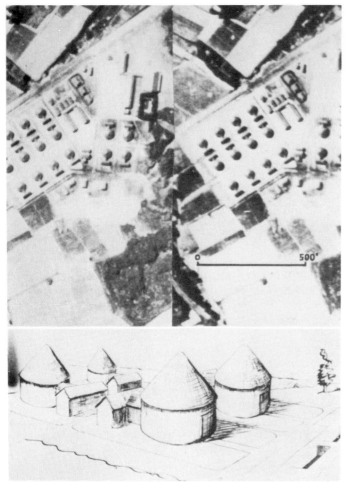

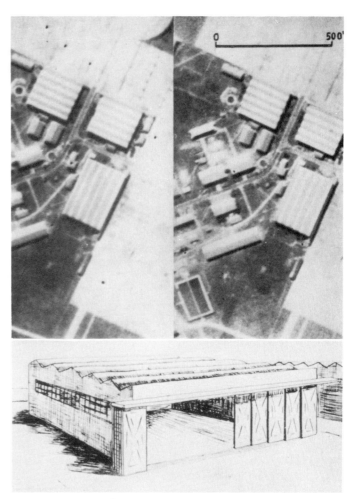

PREFABRICATED BARRACKS are shown at Tainan. They are north of the airfield. Tainan, shown in IMPACT, Vol. II, No. 2, is a fairly new field and is still undergoing expansion.

SAW-TOOTHED ROOF HANGAR-SHOPS are at Okayama, major base on Formosa, north of Takao. An aircraft assembly plant makes this a "flyaway" point as well as a staging area.

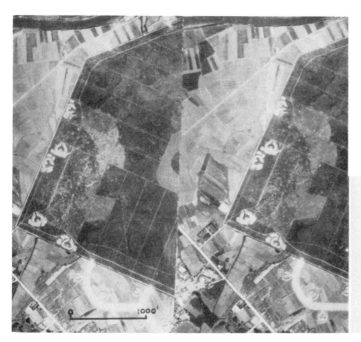

GASOLINE TRUCK SHELTER, not shown in a stereo pair, is partly underground at Shinchiku. Similar to those reported in Burma, these are of more permanent construction.

LYRE-SHAPED REVETMENTS AT OKAYAMA HOLD THREE FIGHTERS EACH

'On the Deck' Tactics by French in A-20s

French fliers of the Allied Expeditionary Air Force are masters of the kind of quick-breaking attack pictured here. Flying American A-20s, they make hit-and-run forays into France, Holland and Belgium, operating from English bases. Favorite targets are airfields and scattered industrial installations too small to be worth a high-level visit from heavy bombers. These photographs are from an AAF combat film taken during a minimum-altitude mission. They illustrate two points characteristic of these operations: freedom from fighter interception and exposure to light flak during the target run. They also lend some substance to the myth that the low-flying French pilot finds his way over France by recognizing his own chickens.

1. CROSS OF LORRAINE, Free French emblem, is used in squadron device. Marking (below) is reverse of British.

2. LEAVING ENGLISH COAST, with cliffs of Dover in background, A-20s skim over water at from 100 to 300 feet.

3. IN MID-CHANNEL planes fly even lower. Fighters cannot dive without risking a crash; radar detection is avoided.

4. AT FRENCH COAST fliers climb slightly to get over the cliffs. Landfall strips (IMPACT Vol. II, No. 2) are useful.

5. SHADOW LOOMS LARGE 20 feet above treetops. Planes fly straight course, climb over obstacles rather than around.

6. DOWN MAIN STREET of a French village—note grass plots in center of road, signpost and two pedestrians.

7. BRIEFED FOR ANOTHER TARGET, flier ignores large factory, clears chimneys with inches to spare, returns on deck.

8. APPROACHING TARGET, already hit, plane climbs 200-500 feet to bomb. White flashes are from four AA batteries.

9. OVER TARGET, plane flies through smoke of previous bursts to escape flak. Guns (flashes at right) keep shooting.

GAS CAPACITY,

Deep penetration into Germany forces our bombers to fly through an increasingly thick and desperate net of German intercepters. The pictures on this page, from the Eighth Air Force film, "Ramrod to Emden," show scenes from an escort mission flown by P-47s. Emden, being on the coast, can be attacked from the sea, and fighter protection is needed only at the target. Fighter escort is needed all the way, however, on longer missions. This has presented the Eighth Fighter Command with an extremely

1. P-47 carries single external gas tank which holds maximum of 108 gallons.

2. No time is lost taxiing. This picture shows eight planes, all in motion.

3. Flare is fired to start take-offs. Note planes waiting around edge of field.

4. Take-off is by twos. On wide grass fields, sixteen can get off at once.

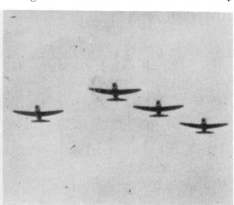

5. First pair is joined by second, which has climbed faster, turned sharper.

6. Squadron is now complete. It will fly this tight formation to rendezvous.

7. At rendezvous, one squadron goes high. Others maneuver with bombers.

8. Fighters keep away from bombers, avoid pointing noses directly at them.

9. P-47 chases FW-190. Latter is supposed to avoid dogfights, go for bombers.

10. FW-190 fails to penetrate fighter cover, goes down, both wingtips smoking.

11. Returning P-47s peel off swiftly to land. Their gas tanks are nearly empty.

TIMING CHIEF FACTORS IN LONG RANGE ESCORT

complex problem. Fighter range is short, especially at the high speeds required over enemy territory. If adequate escort is to be provided, groups must be sent out from scattered airfields on a split-second schedule. Successive rendezvous points along the bomber route will then be hit on the nose, leaving no gaps for gang-up attacks by the enemy.

Less obvious but equally important is efficient take-off and assembly, such as the procedure illustrated below for a squadron of P-51s from an airfield with

a narrow runway in England.

After receiving the field order on a given operation, showing him where and when his group will rendezvous, the Group Commander figures the take-off time of his planes. This is done in terms of gas capacity and consumption, cruising speed, and time spent assembling. The latter is the only variable and has been reduced to a minimum to provide extra minutes over Germany instead of extra minutes circling the home field while waiting for "Slow Joe" to join up.

After gassing up, all planes are taxied into position before any leave the field. Take-off is in pairs, the formation commander being the first off. He circles the field in a slow climbing turn, to be joined as soon as possible by a second pair which takes off the instant he clears the runway. Now leading a flight of four planes, he slowly climbs and turns until the three succeeding flights have formed and fallen into place behind him. Rendezvous with the other squadrons is made at a predetermined altitude.

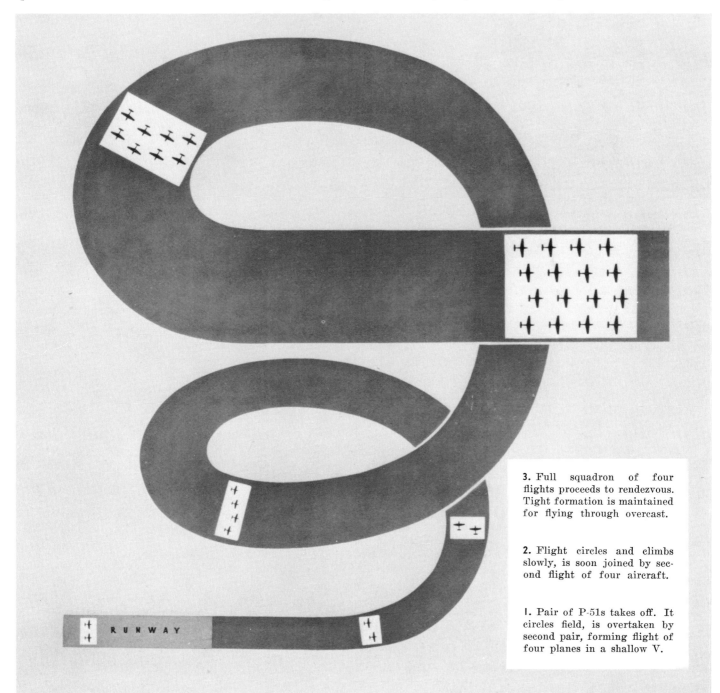

3. Full squadron of four flights proceeds to rendezvous. Tight formation is maintained for flying through overcast.

2. Flight circles and climbs slowly, is soon joined by second flight of four aircraft.

1. Pair of P-51s takes off. It circles field, is overtaken by second pair, forming flight of four planes in a shallow V.

Continued on next page

PLAN AND RESULTS

A glance at the general plan for a large-scale bombing and escort mission (the operation of 11 January, shown at right) indicates the complexity of the 8th Fighter Command's problem: to provide escort for a 200-mile-long procession of 720 bombers flying over 280 miles of heavily defended enemy territory to Oschersleben, Brunswick and Halberstadt.

Previous German reaction indicated little interception at the coast, violent attacks over the target and just beyond. Accordingly, the available force of about 600 fighters was split up as follows: Extreme-range P-51s got a target assignment. A thick withdrawal cover, to protect the expected crop of cripples, was worked out for the P-38s and P-47s, with remaining P-47 groups assigned to penetration. This arrangement produced overlapping at anticipated hot spots, gaps at others. A Typhoon sweep was planned to draw off enemy fighters in Belgium and Northern France. Some Spitfires, not indicated on chart, were to help cripples across the channel.

Although weather and other factors interfered with carrying out this mission exactly as planned, results indicate that the long range escort contributed to the damaging of vital fighter factories at Oschersleben and Brunswick. We lost 60 bombers and five fighters, however.

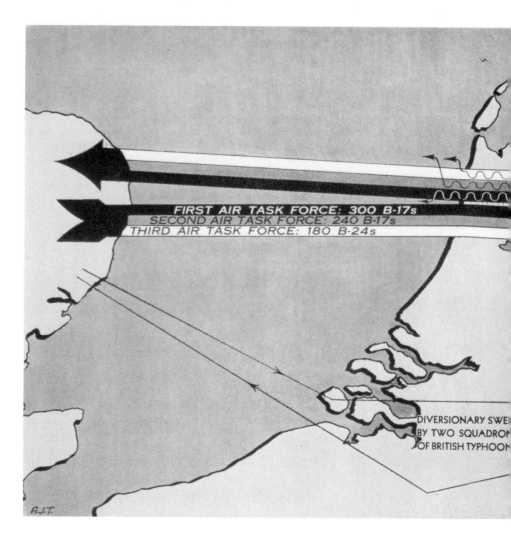

FIRST AIR TASK FORCE: 300 B-17s
SECOND AIR TASK FORCE: 240 B-17s
THIRD AIR TASK FORCE: 180 B-24s

DIVERSIONARY SWEEP BY TWO SQUADRONS OF BRITISH TYPHOONS

OSCHERSLEBEN: Two stages of this attack are shown. In the first, bursts cover the whole FW-190 factory. Obscured by smoke, the main machine shop (A), the main (B) and north (C) assembly shops are afire. Boiler house was hit, too.

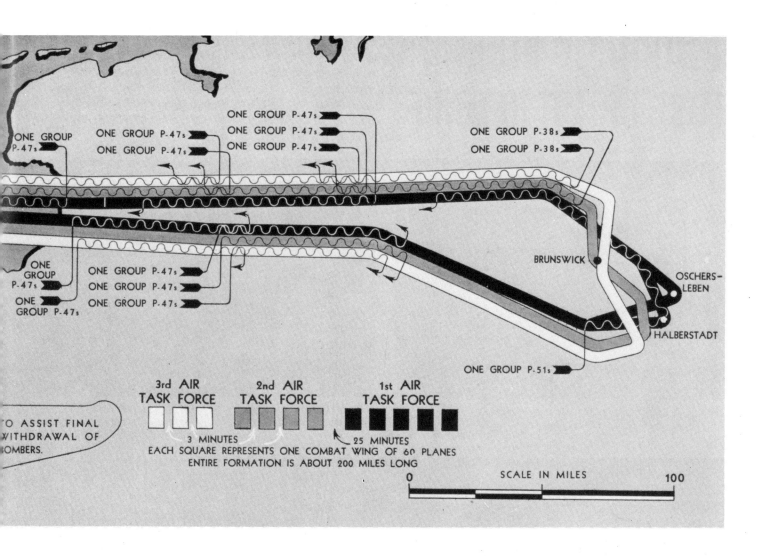

ONE GROUP P-47s
ONE GROUP P-47s
ONE GROUP P-47s
ONE GROUP P-47s
ONE GROUP P-47s
ONE GROUP P-47s
ONE GROUP P-38s
ONE GROUP P-38s

ONE GROUP P-47s

ONE GROUP P-47s
ONE GROUP P-47s
ONE GROUP P-47s
ONE GROUP P-47s
ONE GROUP P-47s
ONE GROUP P-47s

BRUNSWICK

OSCHERS-LEBEN

HALBERSTADT

ONE GROUP P-51s

TO ASSIST FINAL WITHDRAWAL OF BOMBERS.

3rd AIR TASK FORCE
□ □ □
3 MINUTES

2nd AIR TASK FORCE
■ ■ ■ ■

1st AIR TASK FORCE
■ ■ ■ ■ ■
25 MINUTES

EACH SQUARE REPRESENTS ONE COMBAT WING OF 60 PLANES
ENTIRE FORMATION IS ABOUT 200 MILES LONG

0   SCALE IN MILES   100

BRUNSWICK, during and after: This plant, producing Me-110s, was also smothered on 11 January. Damage includes sub-assembly shops partly wrecked (1), assembly severely damaged (2), workshops destroyed (3), offices gutted (4).

0   2000'

RETURN TO RJUKAN: CLOSE-UP OF DAMAGE

On 16 November the 8th Bomber Command made a 1,500-mile round trip to attack targets in Norway. IMPACT, Vol. 2, No. 1, reported this mission, showing aerial views of the bomb damage and pointing out that the job was especially tough because deep snow and deep shadows obscured the targets. Among them was an important electric power plant and

TARGET AREA shows (1) power station, (2) electrolysis plant, (3) penstock. Numbers correspond to those on captions.

1. VERMORK POWER STATION, Rjukan, suffered three direct hits. This disrupted Norway's largest factory system.

1. DAMAGED GENERATOR in power station is one of three put out of commission. Two others were completely destroyed.

chemical factory at Rjukan, about 100 miles west of Oslo. As a follow-up, here are ground pictures of Rjukan, showing bomb damage produced on this same mission. Credit for the attack belongs to 147 B-17s and 29 B-24s. From 12,000 to 14,000 feet they dropped 711 thousand-pound GP bombs, fused at 1/10 second nose and tail, and 295 five hundred-pound GP bombs, fused at 1/10 second nose and 1/40 second tail. Only one bomber, a B-17, was lost in the operation. The big electric power plant was badly crippled. The nearby chemical plant suffered somewhat less, but sustained extensive damage to its nitric fume pipelines, ammonia combustion plant, metal workshop and its transportation facilities.

2. ELECTROLYSIS PLANT, three top floors badly damaged, is world's largest, supplies hydrogen, oxygen and heavy water.

ELECTRO CHEMICAL WORKS, several miles from power plant, producing ammonia, has one of workshops gutted.

3. DAMAGED PENSTOCK contains water pipelines camouflaged by fake trees. Latter are only pin points in aerial picture.

feet to more than 6,000. This field was ready only six days after our landings. This is Hawkins on Betio island, one of two Tarawa fields. Lack of space for dispersal areas necessitates lining up the B-24s and B-25s.

mostly for its heavies, the 7th is now a well-balanced air force.

at right. In spite of precautions like this the enemy does score sometimes.

NINE JAP PLANES found a 200-barrel Tarawa gas dump with 26 out of 36 100-pound bombs. From 11 November to 31 January there were 172 enemy sorties over our bases.

Continued on next page

Working Closer to D-Day

Once the Gilbert bases were ready, the campaign in the Marshalls swung into high gear. An earlier stage of this was

shown in IMPACT, Vol. II, No. 2. The 7th Air Force operations from D—7 through D-day had as specific objectives: (1) From D—7 to D—3, to deny Mille and Jaluit as air bases to the enemy and to destroy aircraft and air facilities at

CANNON-BEARING B-25s were used to good effect, both against shore installations and shipping. They are shown

working over a destroyer or light cruiser sunk at Maloelap on 11 January by 75 mm. fire and one 500-lb. bomb. Note explosion.

ROI FIELD, KWAJALEIN—on 23 January the 7th AF dropped 400 hundred-pound bombs with pinpoint accuracy.

Elimination of radar helped carrier force achieve surprise. In week before D-day the 7th dropped 133 tons on Kwajalein.

Maloelap, Wotje, Roi and Kwajalein—if the field there was operational. (2) From D—3 to D-day. To assist other forces in keeping Wotje and Maloelap inoperative. (3) To attack enemy shipping as a target of first priority at all times during

the period. From 7 December, 1943, to 31 January, 1944, which was D-day for the Kwajalein landing, there were 1,876 bomber sorties, one-third by heavies, during which 1,600 tons of bombs were dropped, two-thirds by heavies.

ANOTHER VICTIM of B-25s at Maloelap, this one, a 5,000-ton cargo vessel, sunk with two 500-lb. bombs on 11 January.

SHORE INSTALLATIONS at Maloelap are hit by B-25s, too. Masthead tactics are like those used in SW Pacific.

ROI FIELD, KWAJALEIN—on 29 January, D—2, Navy planes proceed to knock out remains of Jap air force. When

carriers came into Marshalls aims were to finish pulverizing bases, augment surface shelling, participate in landing.

Continued on next page

continued

Installations Target for Landing Period

BEFORE: Radio and weather station at Rongelap, 110 miles north of Kwajalein, is shown before 7th AF attack.

DURING: On 2 February, four B-24s dropped 160 hundred-pound bombs in 11 approaches, from 8,700 to 1,000 feet.

AFTER a third of the bombs had dropped, the center of the main building was gutted. Of bombs, 93% hit the target.

AFTER six days Navy fliers, who also bombed, took this picture. This helped isolate defenders of Kwajalein.

Continued Attacks Helped Take Eniwetok

HIT ON HANGAR

GUTTED HANGAR

BURST ON OPERATIONS HQ.

BOMB BOUNCING ON RUNWAY INTERSECTION

FOLLOW THE BOUNCING BOMBS—attacks which kept uncaptured Marshall bases neutralized helped amphibious forces capture Eniwetok, not otherwise softened up. These pictures show B-25s hitting Maloelap (Taroa), 13 February.

JUNKED PLANES at Taroa—Capt. R. F. Whitehead, USN, commanding carrier aviation during Kwajalein landing, said: "Carrier forces, because of the 7th's elimination of aerial opposition were able to give their whole attention to attack."

2. DOOMSDAY AT DAGUA, SWPA

A preview of the ultimate doomsday at Dagua is this 5th Air Force minimum altitude attack on a Jap air strip eight miles west of Wewak on 3 February. The leading B-25 (left) unloads parafrags on three Tonys, while other parafrags pepper the strip. Notice the dim B-25 at upper left. At right, a B-25 cuts through dense smoke from a burning Helen.

Continued on next page

5th AF WEAKENS WEWAK TO AID ADMIRALTIES

Repeated air attacks on Jap bases in the Wewak area prior to the invasion of the Admiralty islands on 29 February contributed to the success of the operation. As the Wewak strips are the nearest bases to the Admiralty group, these 5th Air Force attacks deprived the Japs of important support, weakened their whole air defense system.

On 3 February, for example, the Wewak area was hit heavily in the morning by 58 B-24s and 40 B-25s, supported by P-38s, P-40s, and P-47s. The B-25s made minimum altitude attacks on Dagua and But, pictured on these pages, dropping nearly 1,000 parafrags and parafrag clusters. Gas trucks, fuel dumps, luggers and barges were also strafed. None of our bombers were lost. Including those on the ground and in the air, 80 enemy planes were destroyed.

In perhaps significant contrast to Rabaul, which is now important to the enemy only as an outpost, New Guinea is a key point on the main route to the Philippines. Therefore, the Japs are trying to keep up their fighter strength around Wewak, while the AAF, more successfully, is keeping it down. For example, in three days (11, 12, 13 March), the AAF dropped 500 tons on Wewak, destroyed 50 Jap planes.

BOMBING at Dagua is shown in sequence of three pictures. Jap planes are: (1) Oscar; (2) Tony; (3) Helen; (4) Lily. Unserviceable planes are marked US. Note falling parafrags.

RUN CONTINUES, revealing more of drainage ditches, revetments, slit trenches. Picture below shows final stage of run. Black smoke from burning Helen is shown on page 25.

HIT: ONE FUEL TRUCK, which catches fire as 5th AF planes strafe the strip. Camouflage awnings for planes beneath trees only seem to make them more conspicuous here.

AT BUT, the 3 February mission provided a close view of six 20 mm. A/A guns (arrows), heavily revetted in a garden near two observation posts. Over hills Dagua burns.

MOMOTE FIELD on Los Negros island in the Admiralty group is now our base, won partly because of Wewak attacks. Runway can be lengthened at left for heavies.

5TH AF SMOKE BOMBS HIT CAPE GLOUCESTER AREA

BOMB AT FAR LEFT EXPLODES TOO LOW TO SPREAD

PHOSPHORUS BOMBS DO DUTY FOR BOTH AAF AND THE JAPS

Phosphorus bombs, used in the Pacific by both the AAF and the Japs, serve a double purpose: to provide smoke cover and to start fires. The four photos above were taken from an AAF movie and show how our WP bombs provided cover on 25 December for 5th AF bombing operations on Cape Gloucester, preceding our landing there on the next day. The smoke effectively blanketed Jap gun positions on Target Hill and along the coast, making it difficult to attack our bombers from the ground. Upon explosion, the WP bomb emits particles of burning phosphorus which spray out in all directions, leaving trails of white smoke. These bombs are generally fused to explode from 50 to 100 feet above the ground, which permits the spidery smoke trails to spread a maximum distance. At the far left of the photo directly above you see one bomb which failed to detonate until striking the ground, thus reducing the spread of smoke. Phosphorus bombs have proved very efficient, especially in limited areas like the South Pacific Islands, as smoke cover for enemy A/A and to screen our own troop movements. Their incendiary effect is secondary. The Japs, however, are using phosphorus in incendiary bombs dropped from aircraft. Such bombs, fused to explode in the proximity of our formations, are intended to set our planes afire. So far they have not done much damage. It is also possible that aerial phosphorus bombs are used as rallying points for Jap fighters. A specific example of Jap aerial bombing, which took place on 27 January, is shown below.

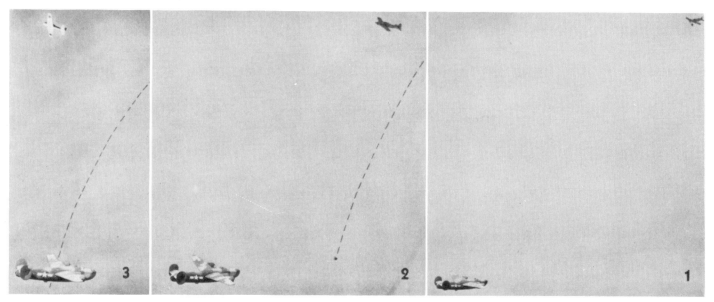

AIR-TO-AIR BOMBING ATTACK by a Jap Hamp on a B-24 in western New Guinea is illustrated with models. The Hamp levels off (1) not far above B-24 and releases aerial bomb too soon. In (2) bomb goes down in front of the B-24. At left, bomb has fallen harmlessly below the Liberator and Hamp has pulled up to come around for a second attack.

SMOKE OBSCURES JAP A/A GUNS ON TARGET HILL

SMOKE HIDES OUR PLANES FROM JAP COASTAL A/A

AIR-TO-AIR—Jap phosphorus bombs bursting over Vuna-kanau, one of Rabaul's airfields, are photographed from a B-25. At left is another B-25 of same squadron. Zekes carry two or three such bombs on each plane, pull up sharply and release bomb, thus hurling it some distance. Pilots describe bombs as more of a "harassing agent" than a real menace.

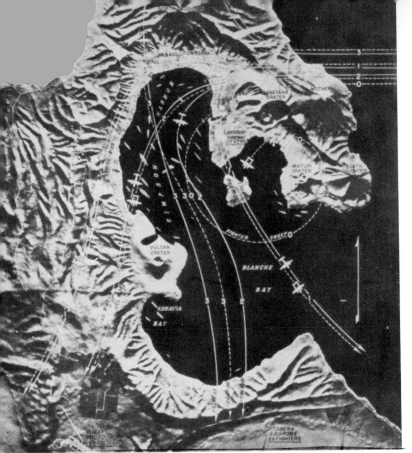

TACTICS of attack on Rabaul shipping by 5th AF on 2 November is shown on these two maps. Above, (O) indicates the two squadrons assigned to the fighter sweep of harbor three minutes before bombardment; (1) indicates fighters and bombers neutralizing shore and AA positions by smoke, strafing fire and bombs—four bombardment squadrons participated in the attack, while two fighter squadrons provided close cover; (2) indicates two squadrons leading assault against harbor—another fighter squadron provided close cover; (3) indicates route of three bomber squadrons which attacked harbor about four minutes after the two leading elements had completed their mission. Below is a compilation of Jap ship losses.

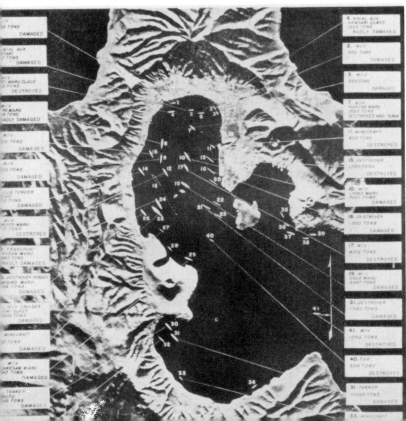

Toward Truk and Beyond . . .

3. ALTITUDE BOMBING BY THE 13th WRITES EPITAPH FOR RABAUL

In the reduction of Rabaul from a great Jap stronghold to what is now barely a toehold, the Air Forces have played a major part, employing a succession of tactical methods. By 2 November the 5th Air Force's relentless low level attacks had all but driven Jap heavy shipping from the harbor. On 23 December the new 13th Air Force, operating under General Harmon's USFASIPA, which in turn is under Navy Command, began its continuous high altitude strikes on Rabaul's airfields. These tactics served the even more important purpose of luring Jap fighters into the air, and involved the type of combined Navy, Marine and AAF fighter escort illustrated on the opposite page.

In January, out of 627 Jap fighters destroyed in the entire South Pacific area, 458 were downed in aerial combat over Rabaul alone. A turning point in these operations took place on 27 January when for the first time Jap fighters over Rabaul refused combat. Since then they have sporadically returned to fight. Specifically, since 17 February little, if any, aerial defense has been offered by the enemy.

He did send up 6-8 fighters on 28 February, but again they refused combat—a minor fact worth mentioning because it stands for a major victory.

The total absence of interference has permitted our aerial forces to sweep at will over the target, even resorting to fighter-bomber and strafing runs. Because of this new development, our forces have switched over to the town area as a primary target (see page 32). Knockout blows are now being aimed at installations, supplies and ammunition dumps in an effort to reduce to a minimum all means of supplying the ground forces, which appear to be the only substantial enemy elements remaining at the once powerful base.

P-38 ESCORT used for 13th AF high altitude bombing climbs to position. This frame from an AAF movie shows semi-plan view. This was a February mission.

Continued on page 32

26000′

24,000

Typical 13th AF Formation

A typical 13th Air Force formation of heavy bombers with an AAF-Navy-Marine fighter escort is shown head-on in this diagram. Bomber and fighter silhouettes and formations are to scale, but wavy lines indicate where full altitude between elements has been omitted in order to show the entire formation within the limits of this page. Each element of three B-24s is flying in V formation on the same horizontal level. Behind the foremost and topmost element, each V is stepped down about 100 feet. The fighter escort of F4Us and P-38s scissors back and forth above the bombers. Each element consists of four planes in the standard formation as shown in the movie frame at the left.

22,000′

21,000′

20.000′

AT RABAUL SHIPS DESERT THE RATS

In contrast to the crowded appearance of Rabaul's harbor on the preceding page is the photograph opposite showing the same harbor taken from 35,000 feet on 7 February. This peaceful, vacant expanse is a direct consequence of low-level attacks which removed from the harbor all merchant vessels above 1,000 tons (except for two wrecks), leaving little else but a flock of barges. The resultant change of tactics to high-level bombing of Rabaul's airfields at Lakunai and Rapopo is illustrated here.

▼ AT RAPOPO on 28 February six B-24s and 10 F4Us make strip unserviceable with 15 direct hits. No enemy aircraft were met.

▲ TOWN OF RABAUL is bombed on 2 March by all-star cast of 48 SBDs, 24 TBFs, 16 P-40s and 24 B-25s, dropping 1,000-lb. bombs from 12,000 feet on Customs Wharf. Since 20 February town is primary target.

▼ AT LAKUNAI on 13 February separate areas are assigned to 23rd and 31st Bomb Squadrons. Of 23 B-24s attacking from 19,000 feet, 16 were damaged by accurate A/A. Pilots of fighters reported bombing "best yet."

PALAO MARU
AK - 380'

"EMILY"

N

1000 500 0 1000 2000 3000
SCALE IN FEET

RABAUL TOWN, HARBOR AND LAKUNAI FIELD
7 February, 1944

10 BLDGS DAMAGED

FIGHTER STRIP
UNSERVICEABLE

BOMBER STRIP
VERY ROUGH

ATAGO
MARU

II SSF

20 SMALL BLDGS
EITHER DAMAGED O
DESTROYED
10 LARGE BLDGS
DAMAGED

F/P

TRUK

MARINE RECONNAISSANCE AND NAVY BOMBING POINT THE WAY TO CAROLINES

The veil of secrecy—which, photographically at least, covered the Jap base in the Truk islands—was lifted on 4 February by Marine Liberators. At the right is part of the mosaic which resulted from that historic reconnaissance. The immediate result was the Navy carrier blows of 16 and 17 February. The 7th Air Force's first blow, which followed, was a 2,100-mile round trip, but we are getting closer and our capabilities do not limit us to attack from one direction, either.

Truk and the other Caroline islands differ from the coral atolls of the Marshalls and from the jungle islands farther south. There is a coral fringe, but where in the Marshalls there is simply a lagoon in the Carolines there are hilly islands (see map, lower right). By the time of the Navy bombing Truk was apparently no longer a base of the main Jap fleet although empty torpedo nets observed on 4 February indicated that the big ships had been there comparatively recently. It did turn out to be a good place to catch parts of the dwindling surface and air fleet in our campaign of attrition.

Of two main anchorages, one is off the west coast of Dublon (mostly naval) and the other south and east of Eten. A total of 30 naval and 30 merchant ships, 133,700 tons, is pictured at right in harbor, including the battleship shown here on one other. Air strips of more than 4,000 feet each were reported on Moen, Eten and Param islands and seaplane bases on Dublon and Moen. There were 85 planes on Eten, 30 at the Dublon seaplane base and 26 observed at the Dublon plane repair or assembly plant. On the two aircraft carriers (CVs), there were 43, piled in such a way as to indicate that they were being shipped out to the combat zone from Japan proper.

The effect of our Pacific advances, from east, south and southwest, has been to make Truk and other former major bases merely part of the most advanced line, as shown by the map below, taken from the Southwest Pacific Weekly Intelligence Summary.

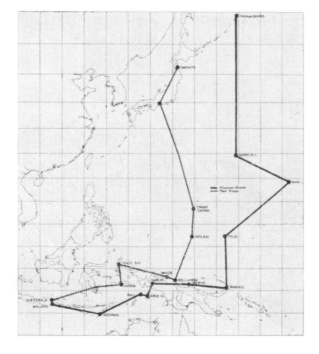

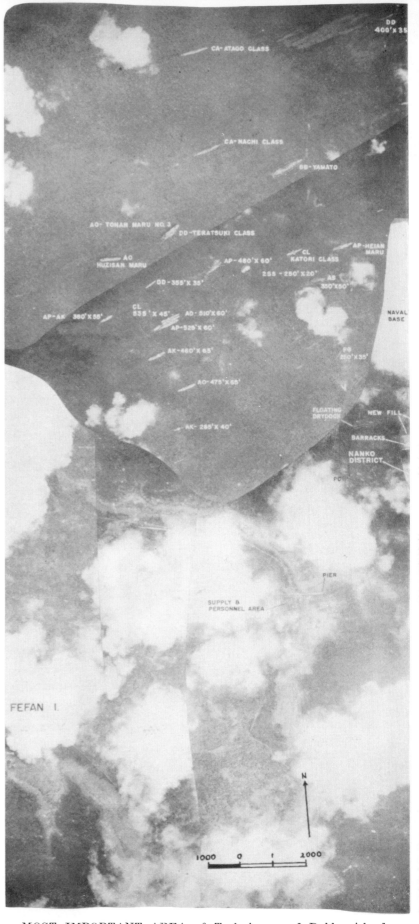

MOST IMPORTANT AREA of Truk is around Dublon island. Installations crowd the shore because of the sharply rising hills (see map and next page). There are 200 buildings in the personnel area,

DD-400'X 35'

A (PROBABLY
ATAGO CLASS)

DD
355'X 35'

DUBLON I.

RESIDENTIAL AREA

HOSPITAL AREA

RESIDENTIAL AREA

Lavalol Bay

RADAR OR RADIO TOWER

BARRACKS AND
PERSONNEL AREA

LOOSE STORES

3 HEAVY AA

WAREHOUSE AREA

BARGE BASIN

AO
HOYO MARU

AO
KAIZYO MA

DD
MUTSUKI CLASS

YO
200'X 35'

AP-AK
370'X 60'

AK-AP 360' X 60'

AK-360' X 50'

EXCAVATIONS

INDUSTRIAL AREAS

TANK FARM

Dublon
Harbor

AK
320'X 50'

AP-AK
326' X 45'

POWERHOUSE

SENDAI
CL

TUNNEL ENTRANCE

PLANE ASSEMBLY
AREA

FUEL PIER

AK-420'X 55'

NAGARA MARU CLASS
460' X 55'

AK
440'X 55'

AH - 267'X 50'

SEAPLANE BASE

CRANE

TAISYO MARU
440' X 55'

SHOPS &
WAREHOUSES

Eten
Anchorage

AK-295' X 50'

BARRACKS

ETEN I.

4100' X 570'

CM-355' X 47'

2 CD
GUNS

AK- AP
TOSAN MARU
500' X 62'

DISPERSAL AREA &
REVETMENTS

AK-AP
450'
X 65'

AP-535'X70'

AO-545'X 70'

AP
NITTA
MARU

CV
645' X 60'

FUBUKI
DD

CV-680' X 80'

DD-ASASHIO

including 18 barracks. In the warehouse area there is 250,000 square feet of storage space in 300 buildings.

OBLIQUE MAP of Truk islands was prepared by the U. S. Geological Survey. Moen (Spring), Dublon (Summer), Fefan (Autumn) and Uman (Winter) are named after the seasons and the islands around Tol after days of the week.

Continued on next page

MORE OF SAME DUE FROM NAVY, 7th AF

STRONG NAVY CARRIER FORCE attacked Truk on 16 and 17 February. Above Dublon seaplane base is hit by incendiaries, with frags on the way down. Note planes.

AMMUNITION SHIP blows up—seen from departing Dauntless dive bomber. Eten island is at right. On the two days 26 ships were sunk, with 19 more probables.

HELLCAT is shown over a smoking Jap destroyer. We lost 17 planes at Truk.

PANORAMA of both anchorages, with ships burning, is shown on 16 February. The toll included 127 enemy planes destroyed in air and 74 on surface out of 272 observed, also barracks, fuel and ammunition. Compare this scene with preceding page.

The 7th Air Force is moving into the Carolines. In the month following 14 February more than 300 tons of bombs were dropped in repeated missions against Kusaie and Ponape. The Carolines and the Marianas were first hit by Navy planes but when the heavy land-based bombers arrive the Japs know they are in for a steady pounding, as they were in the Marshalls (see p. 12). Weather promises to be a major enemy in the Carolines, Ponape (below) is in the Northeast trade winds area and 300 days a year are rainy. February and March are two of the best months, however, for bombing.

WELL-TILLED Marianas, where Navy attacked Saipan and Tinian (above) fields on 23 February, are contrast to atolls.

PONAPE'S topography is indicated below in photo on 25 February, when Langar island seaplane base (1) was afire.

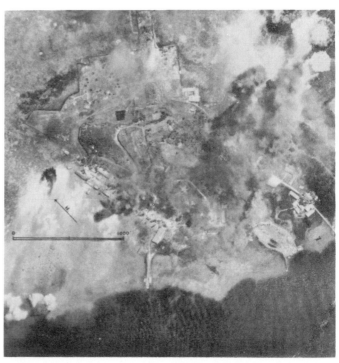

SEAPLANE BASE on Langar island is covered with 7th AF bombs. This attack was from 12,000 feet on 28 February.

Ponape town (2) is on Ponape island itself, where peaks reach 2,600 feet. The airfield (3) has two runways forming an X.

PUZZLE PICTURES

Can You Tell What Is in These

Aerial Photographs?

(TURN THE PAGE FOR ANSWERS)

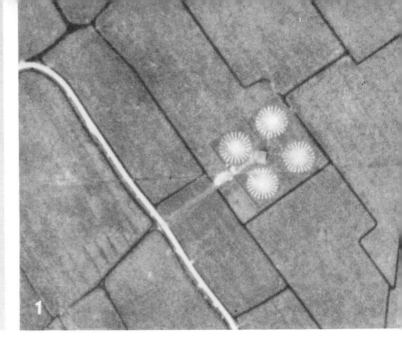

1

4

5

8

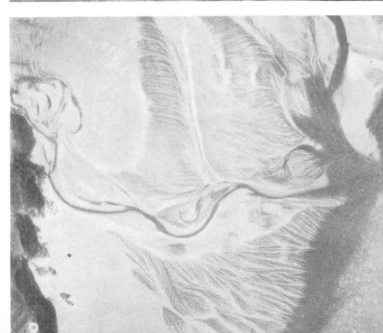

9